ALL SHALL BE WELL

ALL SHALL

HOPE AND INSPIRATION FROM

GREAT CATHOLIC THINKERS

BE WELL

Jane Cavolina *and*

Matthew Bunson

BERKLEY BOOKS, NEW YORK

B

A Berkley Book
Published by The Berkley Publishing Group
A division of Penguin Group (USA) Inc.
375 Hudson Street, New York, New York 10014

This book is an original publication of The Berkley Publishing Group.

Copyright © 2004 by Jane Cavolina and Matthew Bunson
Book design by Tiffany Estreicher
Cover design by George Long

First edition: January 2004

This book has been catalogued with the Library of Congress

Printed in the United States of America

10   9   8   7   6   5   4   3   2   1

This book is dedicated to my niece,
Stella Beatrice Porter, who is seven years old,
with love from Aunt Jane

To my godsons James and Matthew
—Matthew Bunson

Contents

Acknowledgments

Our gratitude to Barbara Zitwer for her enthusiasm, creativity, and vision; to Martha Casselman and Judith Armenta; and to Denise Silvestro, our editor, for making this entire experience delightful.

A special debt of thanks is owed to the many Catholic saints, writers, popes, theologians, mystics, and poets, without whose genius and faith this book would not have been possible.

There is no other reason for counting yourself religious, except that it says something true about you. Namely, that you are in silent awe of the fact that there is truth at all, around you in the dark when the wind is on your face and the distant cold stars seem to dance on into a background that you cannot see, galaxies beyond galaxies in immeasurable time.

—*Michael Novak*

Introduction

The great Spanish mystic, saint, reformer, and nun St. Teresa of Ávila was once riding on a donkey cart in a rugged part of Spain. One of the wheels of the cart slipped into a ditch, and the future Doctor of the Church was hurled out of her seat and landed right in a thick patch of mud. Rising from the mud and noting the grime that now covered her brown habit, she looked to heaven and exclaimed to the Lord, "If this is the way you treat your friends, it is no wonder you have so few of them!"

The words of St. Teresa are a vivid reminder that even the most devout saints and mystics can have an unusual way of looking at the world and a genuine capacity to say the most surprising things. St. Teresa is only one of thousands of women and men who have lived as Catholics over the centuries and who have offered startling perspectives and words of strength, courage, and wisdom to their own generations and to the generations that followed. *All Shall Be Well: Hope and Inspiration from Great Catholic Thinkers* celebrates these words, prayers, and exhortations by bringing together the most moving, stimulating, sometimes humorous, and illuminating reflections by Catholics over the last two thousand years. We hope that readers will find solace and inspiration in the face of daily troubles, national calamity, and their own often difficult spiritual journeys, and that our choices will touch readers' hearts, ease the travails of everyday life, and, ultimately, help bring them a little closer to God.

The vast number of Catholic thinkers who have been our fountain of wisdom and experience range from towering theologians such as St. Thomas Aquinas, St. Augustine, and St. Teresa of Ávila to largely unknown poets and writers, including Henri Nouwen, Paul Claudel, and Hans Urs von Balthasar, to everyday geniuses like Thomas Merton, Michelangelo, Antoine de St.-Exupéry, and Blaise Pascal. All of them made contributions to Catholic life and thought, but their perspectives reach far beyond the confines of Catholicism.

Although *All Shall Be Well* is inherently steeped in Catholic spiritual insights, it is not doctrinal or theological. It invites readers of all religions to reflect on the words of the saints, poets, writers, and others who offer comfort, faith, and courage to those in pain and doubt and give assurance that somehow, in the words of Blessed Julian of Norwich, "All shall be well, and all shall be well, and all manner of things shall be well."

ONE

Good Works

WHEN YOU FEEL ALONE
IN THE WORLD

Acts of charity, kindness, and forgiveness
—THE BALTIMORE CATECHISM

Good works are the little things—and sometimes the big things—you do to show charity to other people. When you help an elderly neighbor up the stairs with her groceries, you are doing a good work. When you visit a sick co-worker who has no one to take care of him—even though he makes your work life miserable—you are doing a good work. When you give money to a beggar on the street even though you suspect he's a phony, you are doing a good work.

There are a million reasons why we forget the humanity of other people in the hustle of our daily lives. We're exhausted. We're depressed. We're busy. We're worried about money. We have our own troubles that insulate us from one another's lives and feelings. It doesn't seem to matter what we do anyway.

But the down times are the most important times to remember why good works are so important: *They make you feel better*. With one selfless act, you can overcome the things that separate us and make a real connection with another human being. There is a rich reward for this: You'll know you are not alone in the world.

Every time you do a good work, you become more mindful of the people around you. If you keep at it, you'll acquire a habit of mindfulness in everything you do and toward everyone you meet. You might not be able to solve all the world's problems, but you can make a difference in the lives of the people you touch.

Selflessness does more than make you feel good; it makes you a better person. Your good works transform you and offer you the promise of a rich and meaningful life.

A good work is an expression of your love. That is good for everybody.

Remember that nothing is small in the eyes of God. Do all that you do with love.

ST. THÉRÈSE OF LISIEUX

To feed the hungry.
To give drink to the thirsty.
To clothe the naked.
To visit the imprisoned.
To shelter the homeless.
To visit the sick.
To bury the dead.

THE CORPORAL WORKS OF MERCY

Simplicity towards God consists in seeking him only in all our actions.

ST. JANE FRANCES DE CHANTAL

Peace here on earth cannot be maintained unless the good of the human person is safeguarded, and men are willing to trust each other and share their riches of spirit and talent.

GAUDIUM ET SPES

Remember that the Christian life is one of action; not of speech and daydreams. I intend every moment of time past, present, and future be employed by me and all creatures in the best way. In heaven we shall rest.

ST. VINCENT PALLOTTI

The Christian ideal has not been tried and found wanting. It has been found difficult and left untried.

G. K. CHESTERTON

He that hath abundance, let him quicken himself to mercy and generosity; he that hath art and skill, let him do his best to share the use and the utility thereof with his neighbor.

POPE SYLVESTER II

Lord, make me an instrument of your peace.
Where there is hatred, let me sow love.
Where there is injury, pardon.
Where there is doubt, faith.
Where there is despair, hope.
Where there is sadness, joy.
Divine Master, grant that I may not so much seek to be consoled,
   as to console;
To be understood, as to understand;
To be loved, as to love;
For it is in giving that we receive,
It is in pardoning that we are pardoned.
It is in dying that we are born to eternal life.

ST. FRANCIS OF ASSISI

The value of life does not depend upon the place we occupy. It depends upon the way we occupy that place.

ST. THÉRÈSE OF LISIEUX

The perfection of the Christian life consists principally and essentially in charity.

POPE JOHN XXII

Blessed are the poor in spirit: for theirs is the kingdom of heaven.
Blessed are they that mourn: for they shall be comforted.
Blessed are the meek: for they shall inherit the earth.
Blessed are they which do hunger and thirst after righteousness:
    for they shall be filled.
Blessed are the merciful: for they shall obtain mercy.
Blessed are the pure in heart: for they shall see God.
Blessed are the peacemakers: for they shall be called the children
    of God.
Blessed are they which are persecuted for righteousness' sake: for
    theirs is the kingdom of heaven.
Blessed are ye, when men shall revile you, and persecute you, and
    shall say all manner of evil against you falsely, for my sake.
Rejoice, and be exceedingly glad: for great is your reward in heaven.

SERMON ON THE MOUNT

Even though knowledge is true, it is still not firmly established if unaccompanied by works. For everything is established by being put into practice.

ST. MARK THE ASCETIC

The bread that you store up belongs to the hungry, the cloak that lies in your chest belongs to the naked; the gold that you have hidden in the ground belongs to the poor.

ST. BASIL THE GREAT

To serve the cause of peace is to serve justice. To serve the cause of peace is to serve the interests of the people, especially the lowly and the dispossessed.

POPE PIUS XII

To admonish the sinner.
To instruct the ignorant.
To counsel the doubtful.
To comfort the sorrowful.
To bear wrongs patiently.
To forgive all injuries.
To pray for the living and the dead.

THE SPIRITUAL WORKS OF MERCY

. . . what good to me was my ability, if I did not use it well.

ST. AUGUSTINE

We should do only those righteous actions which we cannot stop ourselves from doing, which we are unable not to do, but, through well directed attention, we should always keep on increasing the number of those which we are unable not to do.

SIMONE WEIL

It would scarcely be necessary to expound doctrine if our lives were radiant enough. If we behaved like true Christians, there would be no pagans.

BLESSED POPE JOHN XXIII

Inhuman are those who permit human beings to die of hunger while they overfeed their own dogs and horses.

BLESSED CLAUDE DE LA COLOMBIERÈ

Let us unite with those who devoutly practice peace, and not with those who hypocritically wish for peace.

POPE ST. CLEMENT I

Having gifts that differ according to the grace given to us, let us use them: if prophecy, in proportion to our faith; if service, in our serving; he who teaches, in his teaching; he who exhorts, in his exhortation; he who contributes, in liberality; he who gives aid, with zeal; he who does acts of mercy, with cheerfulness.

ST. PAUL

We must not be so insistent upon demanding our rights as in discharging our obligations.

POPE BENEDICT XV

Hospitality is the virtue which allows us to break through the narrowness of our own fears and to open our houses to the stranger, with the intuition that salvation comes to us in the form of a tired traveler.

HENRI NOUWEN

I want to spend my heaven in doing good on earth.

ST. THÉRÈSE OF LISIEUX

Do not honor Christ here in the church with silken garments while neglecting him outside where he is cold and naked.

ST. JOHN CHRYSOSTOM

A man given to fasting thinks himself very devout if he fasts, although his heart may be filled with hatred. Much concerned with sobriety, he does not dare to wet his tongue with wine or even water but won't hesitate to drink deep of his neighbor's blood by detraction and calumny.

ST. FRANCIS DE SALES

Do not let your deeds belie your words, lest when you speak in church someone may say to himself, "Why do you not practice what you preach?"

ST. JEROME

Love of neighbor requires three things: a desire for the greater good for all; to accomplish what good we can when we can; and to hide the faults of others.

ST. JOHN VIANNEY

Riches and power are but gifts of blind fate, whereas goodness is the result of one's own merits.

HELOISE

What we do for ourselves in life is more certain than all the good we expect others to do for us after death.

POPE ST. GREGORY I THE GREAT

Do not show favor only to relations and kin, or to the most eminent—whether they are leaders or the wealthy or neighbors or citizens of the same country. Show favor to all who come to you. By fulfilling your duty in this way, you will reach the highest state of happiness.

ST. STEPHEN OF HUNGARY

Let the wise display his wisdom not in words but in good works.

POPE ST. CLEMENT I

It is not enough to do good things, but we must do them well, in imitation of Christ our Lord, of whom it was written: *Bene omnia fecit*. He did all things well. We ought, then, to strive to do all things in the spirit of Christ; that is, with the perfection, with the circumstances, and for the ends for which He performed His actions. Otherwise, even the good works that we do will bring us punishment rather than reward.

ST. VINCENT DE PAUL

Let the mouth also fast from disgraceful speeches and railings. For what does it profit if we abstain from fish and fowl and yet bite and devour our brothers and sisters? The evil speaker eats the flesh of his brother and bites the body of his neighbor.

ST. JOHN CHRYSOSTOM

If man could see what reward he will have in the world above for well-doing, he would never employ his memory, understanding, or will in anything but good works, without regarding at all what labor or trials he might experience in them.

ST. CATHERINE OF GENOA

No human devices can ever be found to supplant Christian charity, which gives itself entirely for the benefit of others.

POPE LEO XIII

Salvation is shown to faith, it is prepared for hope, but it is given only to charity. Faith points out the way to the land of promise as a pillar of fire, hope feeds us with its manna of sweetness, but charity actually introduces us into the Promised Land.

ST. FRANCIS DE SALES

While you are proclaiming peace with your lips, be careful to have it even more fully in your heart.

ST. FRANCIS OF ASSISI

We should not go to our neighbour for the sake of God, but we should be impelled towards our neighbour by God, as the arrow is driven towards its target by the archer.

SIMONE WEIL

Make many acts of love, for they set the soul on fire and make it gentle. Whatever thou doest, offer it up to God, and pray it may be for His honor and glory.

ST. TERESA OF ÁVILA

With your apostle's life, wipe out the trail of filth and slime left by the corrupt sowers of hatred. And set aflame all the ways of the earth with the fire of Christ that you bear in your heart.

ST. JOSEMARÍA ESCRIVÁ

It is better never to begin a good work than, having started it, to stop.

VENERABLE BEDE

Where there is charity and wisdom, there is neither fear nor ignorance. Where there is patience and humility, there is neither anger nor vexation. Where there is poverty and joy, there is neither greed nor avarice.

ST. FRANCIS OF ASSISI

One must not always think so much about what one should do, but rather what one should be. Our works do not ennoble us; but we must ennoble our works.

MEISTER ECKHART

Virtue is so called because it is something we choose. We choose it and will it in the sense that we do good by deliberate choice and of our own free will, not unintentionally and under compulsion.

ST. JOHN DAMASCENE

Oh, what a pity it is to see some souls, like rich ships, loaded with a precious freight of good works, spiritual exercises, virtues and favors from God, which, for want of courage to make an end of some miserable little fancy or affection, can never arrive at the port of divine union, while it only needs one good earnest effort to break asunder that thread of attachment! For a soul freed from attachment to any creature, the Lord cannot fail to communicate Himself fully, as the sun cannot help entering and lighting up an open room when the sky is clear.

ST. JOHN CHRYSOSTOM

What shall we do brothers? Shall we idly abstain from doing good and forsake love?

POPE ST. CLEMENT I

Do not forget that the value and interest of life is not so much to do conspicuous things . . . as to do ordinary things with the perception of their enormous value.

PIERRE TEILHARD DE CHARDIN

If we want to do something but cannot, then before God, who knows our hearts, it is as if we have done it. This is true whether the intended action is good or bad.

ST. MARK THE ASCETIC

Nothing emboldens the evil so greatly as the lack of courage upon the part of the good.

POPE LEO XIII

Humility must accompany all our actions, must be with us everywhere; for as soon as we glory in our good works they are of no further value to our advancement in virtue.

ST. AUGUSTINE

Do something good for someone you like least, today.

ST. ANTHONY OF PADUA

Do not say: It is impossible for me to influence others. If you are a Christian, it is impossible for this not to happen.

ST. JOHN CHRYSOSTOM

Perseverance

HAVING THE COURAGE
TO SEE TOMORROW

□

Keeping at something until it is finished

—THE BALTIMORE CATECHISM

If despair is being unable to see tomorrow, perseverance is hanging on and waiting for the dawn.

It's seeing the light at the end of the tunnel and knowing that eventually you're going to move out of the dark and into the sunshine—whether you're feeling doubt or fear, illness, grief, or the everyday difficulties of life.

Perseverance is, quite simply, the habit of hanging on until the bad times—or people or feelings—pass and are replaced with better ones. It takes courage, though, because you often can't actually see that light. You just have to believe it's there.

Life's trials often bring profound insights that we might otherwise not have had. If you are distressed, you might become aware of the comfort and love your friends give you, something you might hardly have noticed in normal circumstances. If you or a loved one are ill, you might be brought closer to your family and realize how precious you are to each other. If you are afraid—of losing a job, a partner, or something else you don't think you can live without—you might find that you are stronger than you think. Our tough times can give us a clearer appreciation of the good things we have.

Have you ever felt that there seemed to be a purpose in a past ordeal? The kind of thing it's only possible to see in hindsight? You lost a job, then found a better one; you broke up with a boyfriend, then met your husband. These experiences of persevering through pain build strength and character; most important, when life brings you its inevitable further troubles, they serve to remind you that you have survived tough times in the past and you will survive them again.

A man who governs his passions is master of the world. We must either command them, or be enslaved by them. It is better to be a hammer than an anvil.

ST. DOMINIC

It shows weakness of mind to hold too much to the beaten track through fear of innovations. Times change and to keep up with them, we must modify our methods.

ST. MADELEINE SOPHIE BARAT

Let nothing trouble you
Let nothing frighten you
Everything passes
God never changes
Patience

Obtains all
Whoever has God
Wants for nothing
God alone is enough.

ST. TERESA OF ÁVILA

Time never stands still, nor does it idly pass without effect upon our feelings or fail to work its wonders on the mind. It came and went, day after day, and as it passed it filled me with fresh hope and new thoughts to remember. Little by little it pieced me together again by means of the old pleasures which I had once enjoyed. My sorrow gave way to them.

ST. AUGUSTINE

I am not made or unmade by the things which happen to me but by my reaction to them.

ST. JOHN OF THE CROSS

Have patience with all things, but first of all with yourself.

ST. FRANCIS DE SALES

You need not cry very loud. God is nearer to us than we think.

BROTHER LAWRENCE

God commands you to pray, but he forbids you to worry.

ST. JOHN VIANNEY

Hardly a day passes in our lives without our experience of inner or outer fears, anxieties, apprehensions, and preoccupations. These dark thoughts have pervaded every part of our world to such a degree that we can never fully escape them. Still it is possible not to belong to these powers, not to build our dwelling place among them, but to choose the house of love as our home. This choice is made not just once and for all but by living a spiritual life, praying at all times, and thus breathing God's breath. Through the spiritual life we gradually move from the house of fear to the house of love.

HENRI NOUWEN

Anger is tamed and becomes transformed into benevolence only through courage and mercy; for these destroy the enemies that besiege the city of the soul—the first, the enemies outside and the second, those within.

ST. GREGORY OF SINAI

It is better to limp along the way than stride along off the way. For a man who limps along the way, even if he only makes slow progress, comes to the end of the way; but one who is off the way, the more quickly he runs, the farther away he is from his goal. If you are looking for a goal, hold fast to Christ, because he himself is the truth, where we desire to be . . . hold fast to Christ if you wish to be safe.

ST. THOMAS AQUINAS

No athlete is crowned but in the sweat of his brow.

ST. JEROME

Have patience with all things, but chiefly have patience with yourself. Do not lose courage in considering your own imperfections but instantly set about remedying them—every day begin the task anew.

ST. FRANCIS DE SALES

It is such a folly to pass one's time fretting, instead of resting quietly on the heart of Jesus.

ST. THÉRÈSE OF LISIEUX

Christians must lean on the Cross of Christ just as travelers lean on a staff when they begin a long journey. They must have the Passion of Christ deeply imbedded in their minds and hearts, because only from it can they derive peace, grace, and truth.

ST. ANTHONY OF PADUA

Give yourself in earnest to the acquisition of virtue; otherwise, you will remain always a dwarf in it. Never believe that you have acquired a virtue, if you have not made proof of it in resisting its contrary vice, and unless you practice it faithfully on suitable occasions which, for this reason, ought never to be avoided, but rather desired, sought, and embraced with eagerness.

ST. TERESA OF ÁVILA

There is a kind of simplicity that causes a person to close his eyes to all the sentiments of nature and to human considerations, and fix them interiorly upon the holy maxims of the Faith that he may guide himself in every work by their means, in such a way that in all his actions, words, thoughts, interests, and vicissitudes, at all times and in all places, he may never recur to them and do nothing except by them and according to them. This is an admirable simplicity.

ST. VINCENT DE PAUL

By humble and faithful prayer, the soul acquires, with time and perseverance, every virtue.

ST. CATHERINE OF SIENA

You must be holy in the way that God asks you to be holy. God does not ask you to be a Trappist monk or a hermit. He wills that you sanctify the world and your everyday life.

ST. VINCENT PALLOTTI

Start by doing what's necessary; then do what's possible; and suddenly you are doing the impossible.

ST. FRANCIS OF ASSISI

Dismiss all anger and look into yourself a little. Remember that he of whom you are speaking is your brother, and as he is in the way of salvation, God can make him a saint, in spite of his present weakness.

ST. THOMAS OF VILLANOVA

O religious soul, dove beloved of Christ, behold those little pieces of straw which the world tramples under its feet. They are the virtues practiced by the Savior and thy Spouse, for which He Himself has set thee an example: humility, meekness, poverty, penance, patience and mortification.

ST. ANTHONY OF PADUA

Fear is greater than the evil itself.

ST. FRANCIS DE SALES

Whenever anything disagreeable or displeasing happens to you, remember Christ crucified and be silent.

ST. JOHN OF THE CROSS

Never say to God, "Enough"; simply say, "I am ready."

BLESSED SEBASTIAN VALFRE

First keep the peace within yourself, then you can bring peace to others.

THOMAS À KEMPIS

Restraining my impatience cost me so much that I was bathed in perspiration.

ST. THÉRÈSE OF LISIEUX

Teach us, good Lord, to serve Thee as Thou deservest;
To give and not to count the cost;
To fight and not to heed the wounds;
To toil and not to seek for rest;
To labor and not to ask for any reward;
Save that of knowing that we do Thy will.

ST. IGNATIUS LOYOLA

The more we empty ourselves to make room for God's love, the more he fills us with himself and the more united to him will we be. Many people desire to attain union with God but they are unable to bear the contradictions he sends to them.

ST. ALPHONSE LIGUORI

Hold God's hand on the road of life.

ST. PETER JULIAN EYMARD

Remain at peace regarding whatever is said or done in conversations. If it is good, you have something for which to praise God. If it is bad, you have something in which to serve God by turning your heart away from it.

ST. FRANCIS DE SALES

There is no such thing as bad weather. All weather is good because it is God's.

ST. TERESA OF ÁVILA

Let us pray without ceasing, you for us, we for you; by the love we share, we shall thus relieve the strain of these great trials.

ST. CYPRIAN

Lord my God, Light of the blind, and Strength of the weak; yea also Light of those that see, and Strength of the strong: hearken unto my soul, and hear it crying out of the depths.

ST. AUGUSTINE

·

According to our purpose shall be the success of our spiritual progress; and much diligence is necessary to him that will show progress. And if he that firmly purposeth often faileth, what shall he do that seldom purposeth anything, or with little resolution.

THOMAS À KEMPIS

·

The fact is that no one can climb a ladder in a single stride . . . At the beginning of one's life as a monk one cannot suddenly become free of gluttony and vainglory.

ST. JOHN CLIMACUS

·

Wolves and bears are certainly more dangerous than fleas; yet the former neither give us so much trouble, nor exercise our patience so much, as the latter. It is easy to abstain from murder, but it is extremely difficult to restrain all the little sallies of passion, the occasions of which present themselves every moment.

ST. FRANCIS DE SALES

·

What God asks is a will which will no longer be divided between him and any creature, a will pliant in his hands which neither desires anything nor refuses anything, which wants without reservation everything which he wants, and which never, under any pretext, wants anything which he does not want.

FRANÇOIS DE SALIGNAC FÉNELON

I should like to persuade spiritual persons that the road leading to God does not entail a multiplicity of considerations, methods, manners, and experiences . . . but demands only one thing necessary: true self-denial, exterior and interior, through surrender of self both to suffering for Christ and to annihilation in all things.

ST. JOHN OF THE CROSS

Our heart is restless until it rests in you.

ST. AUGUSTINE

Rest. Rest. Rest in God's love. The only work you are required now to do is to give your most intense attention to His still, small voice within.

MADAME JEANNE GUYON

Ah, fear, abortive imp of drooping mind; self-overthrow, false friend, root of remorse . . . ague of valor . . . love's frost, the mint of lies.

BLESSED ROBERT SOUTHWELL

Perform faithfully what God requires of you each moment and leave the thought of everything else to Him. I assure you that to live in this way will bring you great peace.

ST. JANE FRANCES DE CHANTAL

Any trial that comes to you can be overcome by silence.

SAYINGS OF THE DESERT FATHERS

The offspring of virtue is perseverance. The fruit and offspring of perseverance is habit, and the child of habit is character.

ST. JOHN CLIMACUS

When you encounter difficulties and contradictions, do not try to break them, but bend them with gentleness and time.

ST. FRANCIS DE SALES

One day of humble self-knowledge is a greater grace from the Lord, although it may have cost us many afflictions and trials, than many days of prayer.

ST. TERESA OF ÁVILA

To come to the pleasure you have not you must go by a way which you enjoy not.

ST. JOHN OF THE CROSS

THREE

Love

THE ONE TRUE THING

To like with all our heart and soul

—THE BALTIMORE CATECHISM

The whole system we believe in as spiritual beings and religious people is based on love—in the absolute and in the everyday. Our view of the world and of creation itself as good, as opposed to indifferent, or neutral, or random, or just *there,* is based on love. Love is what makes things *matter.* It's what makes life matter. It's why we say that God is love. Love, indeed, makes the world go 'round—in the most literal way.

The way we are called to behave toward each other is a function of this love: We strive to reflect it in everything we say and do. Love, then, goes hand in hand with responsibility, with a moral imperative to act lovingly toward everyone. We are all equally important in the cosmic scheme as parts of the living whole.

"Whatsoever you do to the least of my brethren," Jesus said, "you do it to me."

Since I began to love, love has never forsaken me. It has ever grown to its own fullness within my innermost heart.

ST. CATHERINE OF GENOA

Love is patient and kind, love is not jealous or boastful; it is not arrogant or rude. Love does not insist on its own way; it is not irritable or resentful; it does not rejoice at wrong, but rejoices in the right. Love bears all things, believes all things, hopes all things, endures all things.

ST. PAUL

God's love for us is not the reason for which we should love him. God's love for us is the reason for us to love ourselves.

SIMONE WEIL

The school of Christ is the school of love. In the last day, when the general examination takes place, there will be no question at all on the text of Aristotle, the aphorisms of Hippocrates, or the Paragraphs of Justinian. Love will be the whole syllabus.

ST. ROBERT BELLARMINE

Give me a heart as big as the universe.

MOTHER CABRINI

I was made of love . . . therefore, in the nobility of my nature, no creature can suffice me and open me, save Love alone.

ST. MECHTILD OF MAGDEBURG

The way to love anything is to realize that it might be lost.

G. K. CHESTERTON

As memory of fire does not warm the body, so faith without love does not produce the light of knowledge in the soul. Whoever entertains in his heart any trace of hatred for anyone, regardless of what the offense may have been, is a complete stranger to the love of God.

ST. MAXIMUS THE CONFESSOR

To love God is greater than to know him.

ST. THOMAS AQUINAS

We are born to love, we live to love, and we will die to love still more.

ST. JOSEPH CAFASSO

If we want a love message to be heard, it has to be sent out. To keep a lamp burning, we have to keep putting oil in it.

MOTHER TERESA

It is only with the heart that one can see rightly. What is essential is invisible to the eye.

ANTOINE DE ST.-EXUPÉRY

In the evening of our life, we shall be judged on our love.

ST. JOHN OF THE CROSS

It is of the nature of love, to love when it feels itself loved, and to love all things loved of its beloved. So when the soul has by degrees known the love of its Creator towards it, it loves Him, and, loving Him, loves all things whatsoever that God loves.

ST. CATHERINE OF SIENA

[It is perverse] to imagine that our enemies can do us more harm than we do to ourselves by hating them, or that by persecuting another man we can damage him more fatally than we damage our own hearts in the process.

ST. AUGUSTINE

Love is not consolation, it is light.

SIMONE WEIL

Without mistakes there is no forgiving. Without forgiving there is no love.

MOTHER TERESA

Let us love God, but with the strength of our arms and the sweat of our brow.

ST. VINCENT DE PAUL

If you keep silent, keep silent by love; if you speak, speak by love; if you correct, correct by love; if you pardon, pardon by love. Let love be rooted in you, and from the root nothing but good can grow.

ST. AUGUSTINE

The truest sympathy is found in those who, with the strength of love, come out of the sunshine into the gloom and dimness of others, to touch wounds tenderly, as though their own nerves throbbed with pain.

ARCHBISHOP FULTON J. SHEEN

All works of love are works of peace. We do not need bombs and guns to bring peace, we need love and compassion. But we also need that deep union with God, prayer. We who have been gathered here for the sake of learning what is peace so as to give it to others, let us learn, let us understand that unless we are full of

God, we cannot give that love, we cannot give that peace to others and we will not have peace in the world.

MOTHER TERESA

Merely to love things that are above is to begin to ascend on high.

POPE ST. GREGORY I THE GREAT

We do not need a peace that will consist merely in acts of external or formal courtesy, but a peace which will penetrate the souls of men and which will unite, heal, and reopen their hearts to the mutual affection that is born of brotherly love.

POPE PIUS XI

The soul cannot live without love.

ST. FRANCIS DE SALES

It is an act of cowardice to seek from (or to wish to give) the people we love any other consolation than that which works of art give us. These help us through the mere fact that they *exist*.

SIMONE WEIL

May my love be the consuming fire, and my yearning desires the breeze that fans it. Let me pour on it the incense and perfume of all virtues, and to this mystical sacrifice let me bring all that I cling to, that I may offer all, burn all, consume all, keeping back nothing for self.

ST. ROSE DUCHESNE

Let love be without any pretense. Avoid what is evil; stick to what is good. In brotherly love let your feelings of deep affection for one another come to expression and regard others as more important than yourself . . . Be joyful in hope, persevere in hardship; keep praying regularly; share with any of God's holy people who are in need; look for opportunities to be hospitable.

ST. PAUL

How sweet is the way of Love!
True, there may be infidelities,
Yet Love knows how to turn all things
to profit, quickly consuming everything
that might displease Jesus,
and leaving at the bottom of one's heart
nothing but deep and humble peace.

ST. THÉRÈSE OF LISIEUX

You must see that no man should be judged by others here in this life, neither for the good nor the evil that they do. Of course, it is lawful to judge whether the deeds are good or evil, but not the men.

THE CLOUD OF UNKNOWING

To fall in love with God is the greatest of all romances;
To seek Him, the greatest adventure;
To find him, the greatest human achievement.

ST. AUGUSTINE

The hunger for love is much more difficult to remove than the hunger for bread.

MOTHER TERESA

Love is essential, so that without love all our efforts are in vain, no matter how much good we accomplish.

ST. ANTHONY OF PADUA

Love takes up where knowledge leaves off.

ST. THOMAS AQUINAS

Better to have loved and lost, than to have never loved at all.

ST. AUGUSTINE

When one is in love, one is humble, one sees oneself as very insignificant, as nothing beside one's beloved.

VENERABLE CHARLES DE FOUCAULD

Love is not to be purchased, and affection has no price.

ST. JEROME

Who can give law to lovers? Love is a law unto itself.

BOETHIUS

To love with understanding and without understanding. To love blindly, and to folly. To see only what is lovable. To think only on these things. To see the best in everyone around, their virtues rather than their faults. To see Christ in them . . .

DOROTHY DAY

⊡

What must be removed from human love—to render it pure, beneficent, universal, and divine—is not the love itself: no, what must be suppressed, or rather surpassed, is the limits of the heart. Hence the suffering—in this effort to go beyond our narrow limits. For in these limits, in our limits, is our human joy.

RAÏSSA MARITAIN

◎

I need to love you more and more, but I don't have any more love in my heart. I have given all my love to you. If you want more, fill my heart with your love.

ST. PADRE PIO

⊞

The Lord sends out his disciples two by two, because the law of charity is twofold—love of God and of one's neighbor.

POPE ST. GREGORY I THE GREAT

⊡

Heart speaks to heart.

JOHN HENRY CARDINAL NEWMAN

It is not necessary to have been well-educated, to have spent many years in college, to love the good God. It is sufficient to want to do so generously.

BLESSED BROTHER ANDRÉ

Let us therefore not cling tightly to structures of thought, but let us plunge into the primal demands of the Gospel, which are also the primal graces, visible, and capable of being grasped in the example of Christ, who gave himself for all in order to save all.

HANS URS VON BALTHASAR

. . . before God made us, he loved us, which love was never slaked nor ever shall be. And in this love he has done all his work, and in this love he has made all things profitable to us. And in this love our life is everlasting. In our creation we had a beginning. But the love wherein he made us was in him with no beginning. And all this shall be seen in God without end . . .

JULIAN OF NORWICH

◎

Love, when it is genuine, is all-embracing, stable and lasting, an irresistible spur to all forms of heroism.

POPE PAUL VI

⊞

The friendship that can cease has never been real.

ST. JEROME

◎

Creation is an act of love and it is perpetual. At each moment our existence is God's love for us.

SIMONE WEIL

◎

. . . put love where we do not find it, and thus will we find everyone lovable.

ARCHBISHOP FULTON J. SHEEN

⊞

FOUR

Suffering

FINDING STRENGTH IN SORROW

Any trouble of soul or body that hurts
—THE BALTIMORE CATECHISM

Suffering—be it physical, emotional, mental, or spiritual—challenges our hope and faith perhaps more than anything else we encounter in life. It is precisely in times of suffering that we most need those virtues, yet it's also when they can feel most elusive. It might seem hardest to believe in a loving God when someone we love is ill or children are starving.

When you're hurting, you can turn inward, angry and bitter, which helps no one, or you can make your trial worth something. You might begin to realize that everyone suffers, and many more deeply than you. Not only can your suffering connect you to everyone around you, but it also can make you more compassionate.

If you can summon the faith to know that joy and goodness still exist in the world and in your own life, you will be anchored by the fact that, even as you suffer, children are born, spring comes, the sun rises, and love surrounds you. The fullness of life always has two sides.

The best thing that can be said for suffering of any kind is that it insists that you sit down and ask yourself the really big questions you always put off asking when life is good. Finding answers to those questions will undoubtedly transform you. A soldier in the sixteenth century was taking part in the siege of Pamplona when he was badly injured by a flying cannonball. He spent months on his back convalescing and had little alternative but to spend that time examining his life. The soldier was St. Ignatius Loyola.

As someone wise once said, "If you can't be brave, act like it. They'll never know the difference." In times of despair, pray, pray, pray. It will help you hold on.

The purest suffering bears and carries in its train the purest understanding.

ST. JOHN OF THE CROSS

It is not enough to be afflicted because God wills it; but we must be so as He wills it, when He wills it, for as long as He wills it, and exactly in the manner in which it pleases Him.

ST. FRANCIS DE SALES

The most beautiful Creed is the one we pronounce in our hour of darkness.

BLESSED PADRE PIO

The extreme greatness of Christianity lies in the fact that it does not seek a supernatural remedy for suffering but a supernatural use for it.

SIMONE WEIL

The scars of others should teach us caution.

ST. JEROME

An iron is fashioned by fire and on an anvil, so in the fire of suffering and under the weight of trials, our souls receive the form which Our Lord desires them to have.

ST. MADELEINE SOPHIE BARAT

Were it possible for us to see further than our knowledge reaches, and yet a little way beyond the outworks of our divining, perhaps we would endure our sadnesses with greater confidence than our joys.

RAINER MARIA RILKE

True followers of Christ: Be prepared to have the world make jokes at your expense. You can hardly expect the world to be more reverent to you than to Our Lord. When it does make fun of your faith, its practices, abstinences, and rituals—then you are moving to a closer identity with Him Who gave us our faith. Under scorn, Our Lord "answered nothing." The world gets amusement from a Christian who fails to be Christian, but none from his respectful silence.

ARCHBISHOP FULTON J. SHEEN

I lived in misery, like every man whose soul is tethered by the love of things that cannot last and then is agonized to lose them.

ST. AUGUSTINE

Each time that we say "Thy will be done" we should have in mind all possible misfortunes added together.

SIMONE WEIL

Jesus was human. He felt pain as we do. And in many ways he experienced pain and suffering more deeply than we will ever know. Yet in the face of it all, he transformed human suffering into something greater.

JOSEPH CARDINAL BERNARDIN

It is necessary to suffer so that the truth not be crystallized in doc-trine, but be born from the flesh.

EMMANUEL MOUNIER

If God causes you to suffer much, it is a sign that He has great designs for you, and that He certainly intends to make you a saint. And if you wish to become a great saint, entreat Him yourself to give you much opportunity for suffering; for there is no wood bet-ter to kindle the fire of holy love than the wood of the cross, which Christ used for His own great sacrifice of boundless charity.

ST. IGNATIUS LOYOLA

The answer to suffering will always be an experience of grace and love.

MONSIGNOR LORENZO ALBACETE

It is often very difficult for poor human nature, oppressed by the weight of sickness . . . to be resigned, to go on believing that God loves it still when He lets it suffer so.

POPE PIUS XII

We rejoice in our sufferings, knowing that suffering produces endurance, and endurance produces character, and character produces hope, and hope does not disappoint us.

ST. PAUL

Our participation in the paschal mystery—in the suffering, death, and resurrection of Jesus—brings a certain *freedom:* the freedom to let go, to surrender ourselves to the living God, to place ourselves completely in his hands, knowing that ultimately he will win out! The more we cling to ourselves and others, the more we try to control our destiny—the more we lose the true sense of our lives, the more we are impacted by the futility of it all. It's precisely in letting go, in entering into complete union with the Lord, in letting him take over, that we discover our true selves. It's in the act of abandonment that we experience redemption, that we find life, peace, and joy in the midst of physical, emotional, and spiritual suffering.

JOSEPH CARDINAL BERNARDIN

If the love of God is in your heart,
You will understand that to suffer for God
Is a joy to which all earthly pleasures
Are not to be compared.

ST. IGNATIUS LOYOLA

O you souls who wish to go on with so much safety and consolation, if you knew how pleasing to God is suffering, and how much it helps in acquiring other good things, you would never seek consolation in anything; but you would rather look upon it as a great happiness to bear the Cross of the Lord.

ST. JOHN OF THE CROSS

By working out our salvation through sufferings, the Son of God has wished to teach us that there is nothing in us so fitted to glorify God and to sanctify our souls as suffering. Yes, yes, to suffer for love of the Lord is the way of truth! Therefore, the more one can suffer, the more let him suffer, for he will be the most fortunate of all; and whoever does not resolve upon this, will never make much progress.

ST. TERESA OF ÁVILA

We have never so much cause for consolation, as when we find ourselves oppressed by sufferings and trials; for these make us like Christ our Lord, and this resemblance is the true mark of our predestination.

ST. VINCENT DE PAUL

There is no more evident sign that anyone is a saint and of the number of the elect than to see him leading a good life and at the same time a prey to desolation, suffering, and trials.

ST. ALOYSIUS GONZAGA

Whatever happens, how could I ever think an affliction too great, since the wound of an affliction and the abasement to which those whom it strikes are condemned opens to them the knowledge of human misery, knowledge which is the door of all wisdom?

SIMONE WEIL

It is tough to watch those we love in pain. But we must believe that by being strong and supportive we make an enormous difference.

JOSEPH CARDINAL BERNARDIN

There is no better test to distinguish the chaff from the grain, in the Church of God, than the manner in which sufferings, contradiction, and contempt are borne. Whoever remains unmoved under these is grain. Whoever rises against them is chaff; and the lighter and more worthless he is, the higher he rises—that is, the more he is agitated, and the more proudly he replies.

ST. AUGUSTINE

Say always, "My beloved and despised Redeemer, how sweet it is to suffer for you." If you embrace all things in life as coming from the hands of God, and even embrace death to fulfill his holy will, assuredly, you will die a saint.

ST. ALPHONSUS LIGUORI

Let the crucifix be not only in my eyes and on my breast, but in my heart.

ST. BERNADETTE

God sometimes allows us to be in such profound darkness that not a single star shines in our skies. The reason is that we must be reminded that we are on earth only to suffer, while following our gentle Savior along a dark and thorny path.

VENERABLE CHARLES DE FOUCAULD

Men owe us what we imagine they will give us. We must forgive them this debt.

SIMONE WEIL

We must forgive the society from which we came; we must forgive the ways it has hurt us. We must have forgiveness for all the pain that we have unknowingly experienced, even in the womb before our birth. We must forgive those who may not have understood us, or have seemingly neglected us, or perhaps even rejected us.

CATHERINE DOHERTY

True patience enables us to bear the misfortune of suffering without incurring the misfortune of sin. Such was the patience of the martyrs, who preferred to endure the tortures of the executioner rather than deny the faith of Christ.

ST. ROBERT BELLARMINE

Poverty requires of us to leave all things and to have nothing of our own. In fact, it consists in desiring nothing but God alone.

ST. VINCENT DE PAUL

Tears are like blood in the wounds of the soul.

ST. GREGORY OF NYSSA

A real pilgrim going to Jerusalem leaves his house and land, wife and children; he divests himself of all that he possesses in order to travel light and without encumbrances. Similarly, if you wish to be a spiritual pilgrim, you must divest yourself of all that you possess; that is both good deeds and bad, and leave them all behind you.

WALTER HILTON

To say that the world is not worth anything, that this life is of no value and to give evil as the proof is absurd, for if these things are worthless what does evil take from us?

Thus the better we are able to conceive of the fullness of joy, the purer and more intense will be our suffering in affliction and our compassion for others. What does suffering take from him who is without joy?

And if we conceive the fullness of joy, suffering is still to joy what hunger is to food.

SIMONE WEIL

I have come to see God's presence in even the worst situations.

JOSEPH CARDINAL BERNARDIN

Let us understand that God is a physician, and that suffering is a medicine for salvation, not a punishment for damnation.

ST. AUGUSTINE

FIVE

Faith

WHEN YOU NEED TO BELIEVE

⊡

The virtue by which we firmly believe
all the truths God has revealed

—THE BALTIMORE CATECHISM

Faith is the grace to believe in what we cannot see. Faith tells us that Colorado is next to Utah even though we've never been there, that volcanoes spew molten lava when we've never been burned by it, that the earth spins on its axis as it revolves around the sun. Faith tells us that God loves the world, that life is a blessing, that other people are as important as we are, that we are capable of being virtuous and worthy of the blessings we receive.

Faith is the most difficult virtue of all, for it asks the intellect to know—not to think—that what we believe is true. Acquiescing to and accepting the existence of the unknowable is the foundation of our religious and spiritual life. If you recognize the beauty and joy of the created world, you're already on your way.

Faith is a gift that comes from outside you, but accepting it requires you to make the proverbial "leap of faith." At a certain point, you either do or you don't. It's your choice. If you can make that leap, you believe.

Your faith is expressed in how you live. It's not enough just to believe. Faith doesn't exist in the abstract; you have to live it out. It is inextricable from good works.

All shall be well, and all shall be well, and all manner of things
shall be well.

BLESSED JULIAN OF NORWICH

Faith seeks understanding. I do not seek to understand that I may
believe, but I believe in order to understand.

ST. ANSELM OF CANTERBURY

Behind the complicated details of the world stand the simplicities:
God is good, the grown-up man or woman knows the answer to
every question, there is such a thing as truth, and justice is as mea-
sured and faultless as a clock.

GRAHAM GREENE

Poor human reason when it trusts in itself substitutes the strangest absurdities for the highest divine concepts.

ST. JOHN CHRYSOSTOM

In the midst of all that diversity there is, however, something which dominates—something which confers its distinctively Christian character on the organism as a whole (as well as upon each element in it): it is the impulse towards the heavens, the laborious and painful bursting out beyond matter.

PIERRE TEILHARD DE CHARDIN

If God is your love and your purpose, the chief aim of your heart, it is all you need in this life, although you never see more of him with the eye of reason your whole life long. Such a blind shot with the sharp dart of longing will never miss its mark, which is God.

THE CLOUD OF UNKNOWING

We are pilgrims and strangers on earth. Pilgrims sleep in tents and sometimes cross deserts, but the thought of their homeland makes them forget everything else.

VENERABLE CHARLES DE FOUCAULD

. . . everywhere you preserve me.

ST. AUGUSTINE

. . . the good which we can neither picture nor define is a void for us. But this void is fuller than all fullnesses.

If we get as far as this we shall come through all right, for God fills the void.

SIMONE WEIL

How glorious our Faith is! Rather than restricting hearts, as the world prefers, it uplifts them and increases their capacity to love.

ST. THÉRÈSE OF LISIEUX

Let me tell you this: Faith comes and goes. But if it is presumptuous to think that faith will stay with you forever, it is just as presumptuous to think that unbelief will.

FLANNERY O'CONNOR

I, alas, am only a poor unfledged bird. I am not an eagle. All I have are the eyes and the heart of one for in spite of my littleness I dare gaze at the Sun on love and long to fly towards it. I want to fly and imitate the eagles, but all I can do is flap my tiny wings. They are too weak to lift me. What shall I do? Die of grief at being so helpless? Oh no! I shan't even let it trouble me. With cheerful confidence I shall stay gazing at the Sun until I die. Nothing will frighten me, neither wind nor rain. If thick clouds hide the Sun and if it seems that nothing exists beyond the night of this life—well, then, that will be a moment of perfect joy, a moment to feel complete trust and stay very still, secure in the knowledge that my adorable Sun still shines behind the clouds.

ST. THÉRÈSE OF LISIEUX

All earthly delights are sweeter in expectation than in enjoyment; but all spiritual pleasures more in fruition than in expectation.

FRANÇOIS DE SALIGNAC FÉNELON

Faith is not a thing which one "loses," we merely cease to shape our lives by it.

GEORGES BERNANOS

Fairy tales are not true—fairy tales are important, and they are not true, they are more than true. Not because they tell us that dragons exist, but because they tell us that dragons can be defeated.

G. K. CHESTERTON

We believe that the Word became flesh and that we receive his flesh in the Lord's Supper. How then can we fail to believe that he really dwells within us? . . . In the sacrament of his body he actually gives us his own flesh, which he has united to his divinity.

ST. HILARY

You alone are always present, even to those who set themselves apart from you.

ST. AUGUSTINE

We are no longer to look upon the bread and wine as earthly substances. They have become heavenly, because Christ has passed into them and changed them into his body and blood. What you receive is the body of him who is the heavenly bread, and the blood of him who is the sacred wine; for when he offered his disciples the consecrated bread and wine, he said: This is my body, this is my blood. We have put our trust in him. I urge you to have faith in him; truth can never deceive.

ST. GAUDENTIUS OF BRESCIA

God's will—peacefully do at each moment what at that moment ought to be done.

ST. KATHERINE DREXEL

If God be for us, who can be against us?

ST. JOHN CHRYSOSTOM

He loves, He hopes, He waits. If He came down on our altars on certain days only, some sinner, on being moved to repentance, might have to look for Him, and not finding Him, might have to wait. Our Lord prefers to wait Himself for the sinner for years rather than keep him waiting one instant.

ST. PETER JULIAN EYMARD

Faith is to believe what you do not see; the reward of this faith is to see what you believe.

ST. AUGUSTINE

Faith furnishes prayer with wings, without which it cannot soar to Heaven.

ST. JOHN CLIMACUS

It is not true that progress, but ignorance, in knowledge extinguishes the faith. The more ignorance prevails, the greater is the havoc wrought by incredulity.

ST. PIUS X

The essence is this: we must begin to live by faith and not by mere "religion." We must have an encounter with God and allow him to enter our very depths. We must remember that God loved us first, and that our religion is truly a love affair between God and us, us and God; it is not merely a system of morals and dogmas.

CATHERINE DOHERTY

We must all undergo a change of heart. We must look out on the whole world and see the tasks that we can all do together to promote the well-being of the human family.

GAUDIUM ET SPES

Let us be generous, remembering always that the salvation of many souls is entrusted to our charity. We can do nothing of ourselves, for we are poor and miserable, but if we have faith and trust in him who comforts us, then we can do all things. Let us open wide our hearts . . .

ST. FRANCES CABRINI

Now, faith is acknowledging a Presence. By now we are used to saying it: Faith is the acknowledgment of a Presence, an exceptional Presence.

MONSIGNOR LUIGI GIUSSANI

Even if I am alone, the word of faith is not weakened for that.

POPE LIBERIUS

If the work of God could be comprehended by reason, it would no longer be wonderful, and faith would have no merit if reason provided proof.

POPE ST. GREGORY I THE GREAT

Faith is the first grace and the source of all the others.

POPE ST. CLEMENT XI

After earth's exile, I hope to go and enjoy you in the fatherland, but I do not want to lay up merits for heaven. I want to work for your love alone. . . . In the evening of this life, I shall appear before you with empty hands, for I do not ask you, Lord, to count my works. All our justice is blemished in your eyes. I wish, then, to be clothed in your own justice and to receive from your love the eternal possession of yourself.

ST. THÉRÈSE OF LISIEUX

My Lord and my God, take from me everything that distances me
from you.

My Lord and my God, give me everything that brings me closer
to you.

My Lord and my God, detach me from myself to give my all to you.

NICHOLAS VON FLÜE

The moment that I realized that God existed, I knew that I could not
do otherwise than to live for Him alone . . . Faith strips the mask
from the world and reveals God in everything. It makes nothing
impossible and renders meaningless such words as anxiety, danger,
and fear, so that the true believer goes through life calmly and peacefully, with profound joy—like a child hand in hand with his mother.

VENERABLE CHARLES DE FOUCAULD

Too late I loved you, beauty so old yet always new! Too late I loved
you! And lo, all the while you were within me—and I, an alien to
myself, searched for you elsewhere.

ST. AUGUSTINE

Three things are necessary for the salvation of man: to know what he ought to believe; to know what he ought to desire; and to know what he ought to do.

ST. THOMAS AQUINAS

Daily, cities hitherto deemed impregnable are captured, men launch out into unknown seas, scientists strive to achieve results vainly sought for three thousand years—yet we pretend it is impossible to become saints, though every day we keep the feats of those who have achieved sanctity.

BLESSED CLAUDE DE LA COLOMBIERÈ

When Scripture says, "He will reward every man according to his works" do not imagine that works in themselves merit either hell or the Kingdom. On the contrary, Christ rewards each man according to whether his works are done with faith or without faith in Himself; and He is not a dealer bound by contract, but God our Creator and Redeemer.

ST. MARK THE ASCETIC

Faith is first of all virtues.

POPE NICHOLAS I

◎

If we make a quietness within ourselves, if we silence all desires and opinions and if with love, without formulating any words, we bind our whole soul to think "Thy will be done," the thing which after that we feel sure we should do . . . is the will of God.

SIMONE WEIL

◎

It is not the actual physical exertion that counts toward a man's progress, nor the nature of the task, but the spirit of faith with which it is undertaken.

ST. FRANCIS XAVIER

◎

What does it avail to know that there is a God, which you not only believe by Faith, but also know by reason: what does it avail that you know Him if you think little of Him?

ST. THOMAS MORE

He departed from our sight, so that we should turn to our hearts
and find him there.

ST. AUGUSTINE

SIX

Hope

LEARNING TO TRUST

⊡

The virtue by which we firmly trust that God will in his
mercy give us eternal happiness and the means to attain it

—THE BALTIMORE CATECHISM

"Hope is the thing with feathers," wrote Emily Dickinson, "that perches in the soul, and sings the tune without the words, and never stops at all, and sweetest in the gale is heard." Faith allows us to believe; hope asks us to trust that there is something to sing about, and to sing on, like Emily Dickinson's little bird, no matter how rough the weather is inside us. It is the grace to see beyond the moment.

Hope is another one of those things we don't need a lot of when things are going well but that is critical when our lives feel meaningless and full of pain. How many times have we felt overcome by despair or despondency? How many times has life again become rich and rewarding? Hope challenges the status quo: Fortitude might get us through hard times, but hope will keep us smiling as we endure them. It enables us to see past today's immediate suffering, sadness, or bad fortune to the big picture. It strengthens us not to lose faith in bleak, painful, or confusing times and assures us that things will turn out for the best.

The most important thing about hope is that it gives us confidence that all the things we believe in—love, compassion, the ultimate meaning of our lives, the essential goodness of man and the universe—are possible. It causes us to reach for the stars. It is, perhaps, the most creative and productive virtue because it teaches us to see what is not there. It is the impulse to see a cathedral in a piece of stone, to see a garden in a handful of seeds, to see the miracle of creation in our own little lives.

I worry until midnight and from then on I let God worry.

BLESSED LOUIS GUANELLA

Hope is a risk that must be run.

GEORGES BERNANOS

I knew nothing; I was nothing. For this reason God picked me out.

ST. CATHERINE LABOURÉ

Patience is the companion of wisdom.

ST. AUGUSTINE

The most hopeful people in the world are the young and the drunk. The first because they have little experience of failure, and the second because they have succeeded in drowning theirs.

ST. THOMAS AQUINAS

We have only to believe. And the more threatening and irreducible reality appears, the more firmly and desperately we must believe.

PIERRE TEILHARD DE CHARDIN

I believe that if a little flower could speak, it would tell very simply and fully all that God had done for it. It would not say that it was ungraceful and had no scent, that the sun had spoilt its freshness, or that a storm had snapped its stem—not when it knew the exact opposite was true.

ST. THÉRÈSE OF LISIEUX

If you want to build a ship, don't drum up the men to gather wood, divide the work and give orders. Instead, teach them to yearn for the vast and endless sea.

ANTOINE DE ST.-EXUPÉRY

So you have failed? You cannot fail. You have not failed; you have gained experience. Forward!

ST. JOSEMARÍA ESCRIVÁ

⊞

We must believe that the Lord loves us, embraces us, never abandons us (especially in our most difficult moments). This is what gives us hope in the midst of life's suffering and chaos.

JOSEPH CARDINAL BERNARDIN

⊡

Yesterday is gone. Tomorrow has not yet come. We have only today. Let us begin.

MOTHER TERESA

◎

It is impossible to go through life without trust: that is to be imprisoned in the worst cell of all, oneself.

GRAHAM GREENE

⊞

Man only escapes from the laws of this world in lightning flashes. Instants when everything stands still, instants of contemplation, of pure intuition, of mental void, of acceptance of the moral void. It is through such instants that he is capable of the supernatural.

Whoever endures a moment of the void either receives the supernatural bread or falls. It is a terrible risk, but one that must be run—even during the instant when hope fails.

SIMONE WEIL

We are firmly convinced that the truths of faith cannot deceive us, and yet we cannot bring ourselves to trust to them; nay, we are far more ready to trust human reason and the deceitful appearance of this world. This, then, is the cause of our slight progress in virtue, and of our small success in what concerns the glory of God.

ST. VINCENT DE PAUL

When one puts all his care on God, and rests wholly upon Him, being careful, meanwhile, to serve Him faithfully, God takes care of him; and the greater the confidence of such a one, the more the care of God extends over him; neither is there any danger of its failing, for God has an infinite love for those souls that repose in Him.

ST. FRANCIS DE SALES

In this holy abandonment springs up that beautiful freedom of spirit which the perfect possess, and in which there is found all the happiness that can be desired in this life; for in fearing nothing, and seeking and desiring nothing of all things of the world, they possess all.

ST. TERESA OF ÁVILA

As for the future, your task is not to foresee it, but to enable it.

ANTOINE DE ST.-EXUPÉRY

We walk in darkness, risking bruising ourselves against a thousand obstacles. But we know that "God is Love" and trust in God as our light. I have the feeling that what is asked of us is to live in the whirlwind, without keeping back any of our substance, without keeping back anything for ourselves, neither rest nor friendships nor health nor leisure—to pray incessantly and that even without leisure—in fact to let ourselves pitch and toss in the waves of the divine will till the day when it will say, "That's enough."

RAÏSSA MARITAIN

The splendour of the rose and the whiteness of the lily do not rob the little violet of its scent nor the daisy of its simple charm. I realized that if every tiny flower wanted to be a rose, spring would lose its loveliness and there would be no wild flowers to make the meadows gay.

ST. THÉRÈSE OF LISIEUX

Many indeed there are who do not think at all—but live in their round of employments, without care about God and religion, driven on by the natural course of things in a dull irrational way like the beasts that perish. But when a man begins to feel he has a soul, and a work to do, and a reward to be gained, greater or less, according as he improves the talents committed to him, then he is naturally tempted to be anxious from his very wish to be saved, and he says, "What must I do to please God?"

JOHN HENRY CARDINAL NEWMAN

Hope always draws the mind from what is seen to what is beyond; it always encourages the yearning for the hidden from what is perceived.

ST. GREGORY OF NYSSA

We must listen to all that God says at the door of our heart.

ST. JOHN VIANNEY

. . . be patient toward all that is unsolved in your heart and to try to love the questions themselves like locked rooms and like books that are written in a very foreign tongue. Do not now seek then answers, which cannot be given you because you would not be able to live them. Live the questions now. Perhaps you will then gradually, without noticing it, live along some distant day into the answer.

RAINER MARIA RILKE

Do not be troubled if you do not immediately receive from God what you ask him; for he desires to do something even greater for you, while you cling to him in prayer.

EVAGRIUS PONTICUS

He who climbs never stops going from beginning to beginning, through beginnings that have no end. He never stops desiring what he already knows.

ST. GREGORY OF NYSSA

Yet we do not despair nor lose heart, because we put our trust not in ourselves but in Him who works in us.

POPE ST. LEO I THE GREAT

The request which arises from the human heart in the supreme confrontation with suffering and death, especially when faced with the temptation to give up in utter desperation, is above all a request for companionship, sympathy, and support in the time of trial. It is a plea for help to keep on hoping when all human hope fails.

POPE JOHN PAUL II

Hope is the knowledge that the evil we bear within us is finite, that the slightest turning of the will towards good, though it should last but an instant, destroys a little of it, and that, in the spiritual realm, everything good infallibly produces good.

SIMONE WEIL

He who works my fate has no need of any other help from me, but the good will to do His Will, and an entire abandonment to His good Providence.

ST. ELIZABETH ANN SETON

Cast yourself in the arms of God and be very sure that if He wants anything of you, He will fit you for the work and give you strength.

ST. PHILIP NERI

Turn yourself around like a piece of clay and say to the Lord: I am clay, and you Lord, the potter. Make of me what you will.

ST. JOHN OF ÁVILA

A rock pile ceases to be a rock pile the moment a single man contemplates it, bearing within him the image of a cathedral.

ANTOINE DE ST.-EXUPÉRY

No human being escapes the necessity of conceiving some good outside himself towards which his thought turns in a movement of desire, supplication, and hope.

SIMONE WEIL

Hope, O my soul, hope. You know neither the day nor the hour. Watch carefully, for everything passes quickly, even though your impatience makes doubtful what is certain, and turns a very short time into a long one. Dream that the more you struggle, the more you prove the love that you bear your God, and the more you will rejoice one day with your Beloved, in a happiness and rapture that can never end.

ST. TERESA OF ÁVILA

SEVEN

Life

YOUR SPECIAL PLACE IN THE WORLD

□

The way we act every day

—THE BALTIMORE CATECHISM

We are lucky to be alive. There is no simpler or more straightforward way to put it. Out of this stupefyingly vast and unfathomable cosmos, life has been granted to us. We are here.

The very fact that we get to partake in this most amazing and wonderful mystery, that we are living and breathing, should fill us with unending delight. It is enough of a reason to celebrate. Every moment of our lives is a blessing.

Each day should fill us with utter gladness that we have the good fortune to get up every morning and do it all over again. This is not always easy to remember—in fact, we often do not feel this way—but it behooves us to make it a habit of mind. Our lives are precious and fleeting, and although at times they might be difficult, life itself is a bounty beyond measure. Being conscious of what we have been given is what we owe our Creator. We express our thanks by appreciating life's boundless goodness, an attitude which has the added benefit of improving our lives.

The urge toward life surrounds us. We see it in the budding of the leaves in spring, the sun coming up every morning, the planet inexorably revolving in its orbit, the fledglings in their nest. "I believe a leaf of grass is no less than the journeywork of the stars," wrote Walt Whitman. "And a mouse is miracle enough to stagger sextillions of infidels."

These things remind us, in the apparently mundane affairs of everyday life, that we are part of a very great miracle, equally so in its grandeur as in its simplicity, in its most significant and its most trivial aspects.

It is fitting that we try hard to do it right.

Men go abroad to wonder at the heights of mountains, at the huge waves of the sea, at the long courses of the rivers, at the vast compass of the ocean, at the circular motions of the stars, and they pass by themselves without wondering.

ST. AUGUSTINE

The earth of which they are born is common to all, and, therefore, the fruit that the earth brings forth belongs without distinction to all.

POPE ST. GREGORY I THE GREAT

Man is created to praise, reverence, and serve God our Lord, and by this means to save his soul. The other things on the face of the earth are created for man to help him in attaining the end for which he is created. Hence, man is to make use of them in as far as they help him in the attainment of his end, and he must rid himself of them in as far as they prove a hindrance to him.

ST. IGNATIUS LOYOLA

One could say that by being in contact with nature we absorb into our own human existence the very mystery of creation which reveals itself to us through the untold wealth and variety of visible beings, and which at the same time is always beckoning us towards what is hidden and invisible.

POPE JOHN PAUL II

My soul can find no staircase to Heaven unless it be through Earth's loveliness.

MICHELANGELO

We know that the world is, in effect, a text, and that it speaks to us, humbly and joyously; of its own emptiness, but also of the presence of someone else, namely its Creator.

PAUL CLAUDEL

A somewhat nervous person once asked me what one can do for peace. I answered: begin by closing doors a bit more quietly!

ST. FRANCIS DE SALES

What place is there in me to which my God can come, what place that can receive the God who made heaven and earth? Does this then mean, O Lord my God, that there is in me something fit to contain you?

ST. AUGUSTINE

It happens that one man eats more and yet remains hungry, and another man eats less, and is satisfied. The greater reward belongs to the one who ate more and is still hungry than to him who ate less and is satisfied.

ST. ANTHONY OF THE DESERT

To make good choices, I must develop a mature and prudent understanding of myself that will reveal to me my real motives and intentions.

THOMAS MERTON

Get away from any man who argues every time he talks.

SAYINGS OF THE DESERT FATHERS

You will find something more in woods than in books. Trees and stones will teach you that which you can never learn from masters.

ST. BERNARD OF CLAIRVAUX

We ought to obey God rather than men.

ST. PETER

The sole cause of man's unhappiness is that he does not know how to stay quietly in his room.

BLAISE PASCAL

Be not anxious about what you have, but about what you are.

POPE ST. GREGORY I THE GREAT

To preserve one's life is a duty common to all individuals, and to neglect this duty is a crime.

POPE LEO XIII

A slight error in the beginning is a great error in the end.

ST. THOMAS AQUINAS

The face is the mirror of the mind, and eyes without speaking confess the secrets of the heart.

ST. JEROME

I have long since come to believe that people never mean half of what they say, and that it is best to disregard their talk and judge only their actions.

DOROTHY DAY

The earth is at the same time mother, she is mother of all that is natural, mother of all that is human. She is the mother of all, for contained in her are the seeds of all. The earth of humankind contains all moistness, all verdancy, all germinating power. It is in so many ways fruitful. All creation comes from it.

ST. HILDEGARD VON BINGEN

◻

Truth never contradicts truth.

POPE LEO X

◎

If you can find a place where God is not,
Go there and sin with impunity.

ST. ANSELM

▣

When the stomach is full, it is easy to talk of fasting.

ST. JEROME

◻

It is not enough for Christian parents to nourish only the bodies of
their children; even animals do this. They must also nourish their
souls in grace, in virtue, and in God's holy commandments.

ST. CATHERINE OF SIENA

◎

Fight all error, but do it with good humor, patience, kindness, and
love. Harshness will damage your own soul and spoil the best cause.

ST. JOHN OF KANTY

Exercise pleasantness toward all, taking great care what you have commanded may never be done by reason of force. For God has given free will to everyone, and therefore never forces anyone— but only indicates, call and persuades.

ST. ANGELA MERICI

True repentance is to cease to sin.

ST. AMBROSE

Can we with justice feel contempt for others and dwell on their faults, when we are full of them ourselves?

FRANÇOIS DE SALIGNAC FÉNELON

Some pursue their own taste and satisfaction in spiritual things in preference to the way of perfection, which consists in denying their own wishes and tastes for the love of God. If such persons perform some exercise through obedience, even though it suits their inclination, they soon lose the wish for it, and all devotion to it, because their only pleasure is in doing what their own will directs, which ordinarily would be better left undone. The Saints did not act thus.

ST. JOHN OF THE CROSS

The life of our flesh is the delight of sensuality; its death is to take from it all sensible delight. The life of our judgment and our will is to dispose of ourselves and what is ours, according to our own views and wishes; their death, then, is to submit ourselves in all things to the judgment and will of others. The life of the desire for esteem and respect is to be well thought of by everyone; its death therefore, is to hide ourselves so as not to be known, by means of continual acts of humility and self-abasement. Until one succeeds in dying in this manner, he will never be a servant of God, nor will God ever perfectly live in him.

ST. MARY MAGDALEN DE' PAZZI

The trouble is that everyone talks about reforming others and no one thinks about reforming himself.

ST. PETER OF ALCANTARA

There is nothing on this earth more to be prized than true friendship.

ST. THOMAS AQUINAS

◻

No one is to be called an enemy, all are your benefactors, and no one does you harm. You have no enemy except yourselves.

ST. FRANCIS OF ASSIS

◎

Control your tongue and your belly.

ST. ANTHONY OF THE DESERT

◻

Beauty is indeed a good gift of God; but that the good may not think it a great good, God dispenses it even to the wicked.

ST. AUGUSTINE

◻

Every beauty which is seen here below by persons of perception resemble more than anything else that celestial source from which we all are come. . . .

MICHELANGELO

◎

God is the friend of silence.
See how nature—trees, flowers, grass—grows in silence;

See the stars, the moon and the sun, how they move in silence . . .
We need silence to be able to touch souls.

MOTHER TERESA

We are not human beings having a spiritual experience.
We are spiritual beings having a human experience.

PIERRE TEILHARD DE CHARDIN

Laugh and play and dash about as much as you like, only be careful
not to say or do anything that would be displeasing to God.

ST. MARY MAZZARELLO

When a man does his work diligently for the sake of God, it is not
a distraction but a thoroughness, which pleases God.

ST. BARSANUPHIUS

It is most laudable in a married woman to be devout, but she must
never forget that she is a housewife and sometimes she must leave
God at the altar to find Him in her housekeeping.

ST. FRANCES OF ROME

Sanctify yourself and you will sanctify society.

ST. FRANCIS OF ASSISI

The more we indulge ourselves in soft living and pamper our bodies, the more rebellious they will become against the spirit.

ST. RITA OF CASCIA

This is the very perfection of a man, to find out his own imperfections.

ST. AUGUSTINE

God has not called his servants to a mediocre, ordinary life, but rather to the perfection of a sublime holiness.

BLESSED HENRY SUSO

You cannot be half a saint. You must be a whole saint or no saint at all.

ST. THÉRÈSE OF LISIEUX

Truth . . . cannot change from day to day.

POPE PIUS XII

Humility is the foundation of all the other virtues; hence, in the soul in which this virtue does not exist, there cannot be any other virtue except in mere appearance.

ST. AUGUSTINE

A friend is long sought, hardly found, and kept only with difficulty.

ST. JEROME

My book, O Philosopher, is the nature of created things, and any time I want to read the words of God, the book is before me.

ST. ANTHONY OF THE DESERT

Sic transit Gloria mundi [Thus passes the glory of the world].

THOMAS À KEMPIS

I live and love in God's peculiar light.

MICHELANGELO

The soul then that has made a decision for God and has given everything to him, catches, from the swamp of voices surrounding it, a sparkle of clear limpid water. It is like finding a sapphire among the rocks, a nugget of gold in the sand. The soul takes this gem, dusts it off, sets it in the light, and translates it into life.

CHIARA LUBICH

Ah! Let us profit from the short moment of life . . . Above all let us be little, so little that everybody may trample us underfoot, without our even having the appearance of feeling it and suffering from it.

ST. THÉRÈSE OF LISIEUX

The world is full of faithlessness, duplicity, and inconstancy; so-called friendship is broken when selfish desires have been fulfilled. This, in short, is what it all amounts to: no human heart ever yet found true and lasting love, happiness, or peace in creatures.

BLESSED HENRY SUSO

We are constantly being pulled back into the false adulthood of our age. Many of us who want to offer consolation experience deep inner desolation. Many of us who want to offer healing and affection to others experience a seemingly inexhaustible hunger for intimacy. Yes, indeed, many of us have lost touch with our identity as children of God.

HENRI NOUWEN

In every one of us, there is hidden, somewhere in the depth of our being, a poet or an artist who is prevented from expressing himself or herself by the everyday tasks. As Baudelaire said, our heart is like a captive albatross on the deck of the ship of life—an awkward, incongruous, ridiculous creature when not in the sky, because it is made for flight and its huge wings prevent it from walking.

HUGO RAHNER

Undoubtedly it would sully this angelic purity, if we were attached to anything earthly, to the love of creatures, and to the satisfaction of being loved by them, of seeing them or other like pleasures, which are unworthy of our vocation, as also are all idle thoughts and frivolous occupations.

ST. JANE FRANCES DE CHANTAL

Do not dwell in any place where you see that others are envious of you. You will not grow there.

SAYINGS OF THE DESERT FATHERS

An unstable pilot steers a leaking ship, and the blind is leading the blind straight to the pit. The ruler is like the ruled.

ST. JEROME

He who is sluggish and weak is by nature bored by a short sermon as much as by a long one, and thinks that things are difficult of comprehension, when they are clear and easily understood.

ST. JOHN CHRYSOSTOM

Among all things that are lovable, there is one that is more lovable than the rest, and that most lovable of all things is life.

ST. ANTHONY OF PADUA

To maintain our soul in a state of peace, it suffices to perform all our actions in God's presence . . .

ST. FRANCIS DE SALES

We have established and developed . . . admirable rules of polity, ethics and justice, but at root, the evil root of man, this evil stuff of which we are made is only concealed; it is not pulled up.

BLAISE PASCAL

When one is already leading an honest and regulated life, it is far more important, in order to become a true Christian, to change the within rather than the without.

FRANÇOIS DE SALIGNAC FÉNELON

Do you wish to be great? Then begin by being. Do you desire to construct a vast and lofty fabric? Think first about the foundations of humility. The higher your structure is to be, the deeper must be its foundation.

ST. AUGUSTINE

Knowing ourselves is something so important that I wouldn't want any relaxation ever in this regard . . . While we are on this earth nothing is more important to us than humility.

THOMAS À KEMPIS

It is not the fault of Christianity that a hypocrite falls into sin.

ST. JEROME

Ecclesiastes declares that there is a time for everything under heaven, and everything may be taken to refer to our spiritual life. If this is so, then we ought to examine the matter; and we should do everything in proper season.

ST. JOHN CLIMACUS

Man, perhaps, understands one truth perfectly: namely, that nothing is understood perfectly.

POPE INNOCENT III

Take good care of yourself . . . have a good appetite. God does not want His friends to look as though he fed them on lizards.

BLESSED RAFAELA MARIA

Living only in the visible world is living on the surface; it ignores or sets aside not only the existence of God but the depths of created being . . . if we look deeper we discover at the heart of things a point of balance which is their finality . . . the heart of man is deep. When we have reached the fountainhead of life in him we discover that this itself springs from beyond. The heart of man is open to the invisible. Not the invisible of depth psychology but the invisible, infinite, God's creative word, God himself.

ARCHBISHOP ANTHONY BLOOM

Better light work that takes a long time than a hard job that is quickly done.

SAYINGS OF THE DESERT FATHERS

God is no idyllic, good-natured, indulgent deity, but a power so mighty that all the terrors of the world are harmless in comparison. What is there about Him which causes Him to put up with us? Why does He not simply wipe us off the earth? Do we not sense His patience, the mighty, deep, serene, forbearing, comprehensive patience which has sway over all things?

ROMANO GUARDINI

The World is a book, and those who do not travel read only a page.

ST. AUGUSTINE

A fat paunch never breeds fine thoughts.

ST. JEROME

If you have men who will exclude any of God's creatures from the shelter of compassion and pity, you will have men who will deal likewise with their fellow men.

ST. FRANCIS OF ASSISI

EIGHT

Death

THE OTHER FACE OF LOVE

The ending of the life of our body on earth

—THE BALTIMORE CATECHISM

Death is *the* inescapable fact of life; we know we are all going to die. The only question surrounding it is how we live our lives in the face of that knowledge. Some people studiously avoid its reality; others acknowledge it and experience a more keen appreciation of the time they have on Earth. Knowing that there is a period at the end of the sentence we call life means every second, every action, every word, every thought counts.

Life is God's great gift to us. The love we have for our lives, for each other, and for the things of this world is not diminished by the fact of our ultimate end, but intensified by it. Love and death are two sides of the same coin: Love gives meaning to our death; death gives meaning to our lives. Together they are the triumph of the infinite over the transient.

Although some people have a difficult time accepting the idea of an afterlife, many believe without question that there is a part of us that will transcend death. Call it what we will—the soul, the spirit, the mind—there is an element of the eternal in man that will, as Lord Byron said, "breathe when I expire." It is the best portion of us that leaves this world behind when we die.

Nevertheless, the loss of someone we love can be one of the most difficult things we have to face in life. Perhaps it is a consolation to know that the pain we feel is part of the love; it is impossible to have one without the other. For the great contentment we experience in loving and being loved, an inescapable price must be paid. And who would have it any other way? We certainly will not give up loving, and we can do nothing to stop death.

As for us, let the thought of our own inevitable death spur us to live our life in a way that is worthy of someone who is destined for immortality.

The great school of living and dying brings us to many an open grave; it makes us stand at many a deathbed before it will be us around whom other people will be standing in prayer.

POPE JOHN PAUL II

If we have been pleased with life, we should not be displeased with death, since it comes from the hand of the same master.

MICHELANGELO

Loss and possession, death and life are one. There falls no shadow where there shines no sun.

HILAIRE BELLOC

O Lord, support us all day long, until the shadows lengthen and the evening comes, and the busy world is hushed, and the fever of life is over, and our work is done. Then in thy mercy grant us a safe lodging, and a holy rest, and peace at last.

JOHN HENRY CARDINAL NEWMAN

As a well-spent day brings happy sleep, so a life well spent brings happy death.

LEONARDO DA VINCI

Our labor here is brief, but our reward is eternal. Be not troubled by the noise of the world that passes like shadow.

ST. CLARE OF ASSISI

Hell is full of the talented, but Heaven of the energetic.

ST. JANE FRANCES DE CHANTAL

Do now, do now, what you will wish to have done when your moment comes to die.

ST. ANGELA MERICI

⊡

Dying loses its speechlessness when it is not reduced to a biological misfortune but is celebrated as a human event. There is no more eloquent proof of the failure of materialism than its panicked helplessness in the face of death.

CHRISTOPH CARDINAL SCHÖNBORN

◎

I wondered that other men should live when he was dead, for I had loved him as though he would never die.

ST. AUGUSTINE

⊞

For myself, I think the greatest happiness in this life is to be released from the cares and formalities of what is called the world. My world, my family, and all the change to me will be that I can devote myself unmolested to my treasure.

ST. ELIZABETH SETON

⊡

You cannot love someone so much that you can prevent that person from dying.

MONSIGNOR LORENZO ALBACETE

A man who keeps his death before his eyes will at all times overcome any cowardice.

SAYINGS OF THE DESERT FATHERS

People are dying every day, every hour, every minute. They die suddenly or slowly. They die on the streets of big cities or in comfortable homes. They die in isolation or surrounded by friends and family. They die in great pain or as if falling asleep. They die in anguish or in peace. But all of them die alone, facing the unknown . . . Dying is indeed a reality of daily life. And yet, the world generally goes about its business disowning this reality.

HENRI NOUWEN

While I thought that I was learning how to live, I have been learning how to die.

LEONARDO DA VINCI

Perhaps the ultimate burden is death itself. It is often preceded by pain and suffering, sometimes extreme hardships . . . if we let go of ourselves—and our own resources—and allow the Lord to help us, we will be able to see death not as an enemy but as a friend.

JOSEPH CARDINAL BERNARDIN

The best way to prepare for death is to spend every day of life as though it were the last. Think of the end of worldly honor, wealth and pleasure and ask yourself: And then? And then?

ST. PHILIP NERI

The horizon at which a human being arrives is like a gravestone: death is the origin and the stimulus for all searching. This is so because death is the most powerful and bold contradiction in the face of the unfathomability of the human question. But the contradiction by no means removes the question. Rather, it exasperates it.

MONSIGNOR LUIGI GIUSSANI

Life is uncertain and, in fact, may be very brief. If we compare it with eternity, [we] will clearly realize that it cannot be but more than an instant. A happy death of all the things of life is our principal concern. For if we attain that, it matters little if we lose all the rest. But if we do not attain that, nothing else will be of any value.

BLESSED JUNÍPERO SERRA

Eternity, eternity, when shall I come to You at last? . . . in eternity where we will love with a glance of the soul.

ST. ELIZABETH SETON

Your mortal body will be refashioned and renewed and firmly bound to you, and when it dies it will not drag you with it to the grave, but will endure and abide with you before God, who abides and endures forever.

ST. AUGUSTINE

A saint was once asked, while playing happily with his companions, what he would do if an angel told him that in a quarter of an hour he would die and have to appear before the judgment seat of God. The saint promptly replied that he would continue playing because I am certain these games are pleasing to God.

ST. JOHN BOSCO

If you will stand firm and grow as you ought, esteem yourself as a pilgrim and stranger upon the earth.

THOMAS À KEMPIS

My life and death are not purely my own business. I live by and for others, and my death involves others.

THOMAS MERTON

The shadow of the cross falls upon each of our lives, although we are not usually aware of it each day . . . the cross has become my constant companion, a reminder of my upcoming encounter with my new friend, death, who will lead me home to God.

JOSEPH CARDINAL BERNARDIN

Every day we are changing, every day we are dying, and yet we fancy ourselves to be immortal.

ST. JEROME

Blessed are those who love you, O God, and love their friends in you and their enemies for your sake. They alone will never lose those who are dear to them, for they love them in one who is never lost, in God, our God who made heaven and earth and fills them with his presence . . .

ST. AUGUSTINE

The fool fears death as the greatest of calamities. The wise man desires it as rest after labors and the end of ills.

ST. AMBROSE

NINE

Prayer

LETTING YOUR HEART SPEAK

◫

Talking with God

—THE BALTIMORE CATECHISM

Many of us turn to God in prayer when we need something. We rarely pray to say thank you and more rarely still to offer honor and praise. This can make us feel a little guilty; it seems as if we only think of God when we're in trouble. But that's all right, because the right frame of mind in which to pray is one of helplessness and dependence—that is, when we know we can't control what's happening to us or those we love and we need God's help. It is, after all, the state of mind in which we're closest to the truth about our lives.

We take a heavy burden off our shoulders when we admit our powerlessness in important areas of our life and look outside ourselves for aid. We are, in return, offered the comfort of knowing that we do not have to bear our difficulties alone. Prayer is, most simply, a way of speaking to God, and the first good thing to come from it is knowing that someone is listening. Anyone who has ever prayed to God, Mary, or the saints in an hour of need knows that this is enormously consoling.

Sometimes we will be given what we desire. Sometimes we will be given the strength to cope with otherwise unbearable spiritual or emotional pain. But we will always be given the knowledge that we are loved.

The habit of prayer—of lifting our minds and hearts to God with regularity, of making a prayerful response to life an integral part of our being—is even more fortifying. It is an anchor in what often feels like a terrifyingly turbulent sea.

The great miracle of heartfelt prayer is that it works.

I pray because I'm helpless. I pray because the need flows out of me all the time. It doesn't change God. It changes me.

C. S. LEWIS

For me, prayer is a surge of the heart; it is a simple look turned toward heaven, it is a cry of recognition and of love, embracing both trial and joy.

ST. THÉRÈSE OF LISIEUX

Prayer is not a one-sided practice.

JOSEPH CARDINAL BERNARDIN

Contemplative prayer in my opinion is nothing else than a close sharing between friends; it means taking time frequently to be alone with him who we know loves us.

ST. TERESA OF ÁVILA

Nothing is equal to prayer; for what is impossible it makes possible, what is difficult, easy. . . . For it is impossible, utterly impossible, for the man who prays eagerly and invokes God ceaselessly ever to sin.

ST. JOHN CHRYSOSTOM

Seek in reading and you will find in meditating; knock in mental prayer and it will be opened to you by contemplation.

GUIGO THE CARTHUSIAN

Grant me, Lord, to know and understand whether a man is first to pray to you for help or to praise you, and whether he must know you before he can call you to his aid.

ST. AUGUSTINE

We should not accept in silence the gifts of God; we should return thanks for all of them.

ST. BASIL THE GREAT

It is essential to begin the practice of prayer with a firm resolution of persevering in it.

ST. TERESA OF ÁVILA

To implore a man is a desperate attempt through sheer intensity to make our system of values pass into him. To implore God is just the contrary: it is an attempt to make the divine values pass into ourselves.

SIMONE WEIL

Just because prayer is personal and arises from the center of our life, it is to be shared with others. Just because prayer is the most precious expression of being human, it needs the constant support and protection of the community to grow and flower.

HENRI NOUWEN

When we are linked by the power of prayer, we, as it were, hold each other's hand as we walk side by side along a slippery path; and thus by the bounteous disposition of love, it comes about that the harder each one leans on the other, the more firmly we are riveted together in brotherly love.

POPE ST. GREGORY I THE GREAT

The reason why sometimes you have asked and not received, is because you have asked amiss, either inconsistently, or lightly, or because you have asked for what was not good for you, or because you have ceased asking.

ST. BASIL THE GREAT

Souls that have no habit of prayer are like a lame and paralytic body, which, though it has hands and feet, cannot use them. Therefore, to abandon prayer seems to me the same thing as to lose the straight road; for as prayer is the gate through which all the graces of God come to us, when this is closed, I do not know how we can have any.

ST. TERESA OF ÁVILA

We can pray perfectly when we are out in the mountains or on a lake and we feel at one with nature. Nature speaks for us or rather speaks to us. We pray perfectly.

POPE JOHN PAUL II

Speak slowly. Think about what you're saying, who is saying it and to whom. Because talking fast, without pausing for reflection, is only noise—the clatter of the cans.

ST. JOSEMARÍA ESCRIVÁ

We can often be distracted, even when we pray. All prayer is a conversation with God, and we need to give him our full attention, otherwise it is like getting an appointment with someone and then day dreaming during the interview.

ST. FRANCIS DE SALES

We can meditate in every place, at home or elsewhere, even in walking and at our work. How many are there who, not having any better opportunity, raise their hearts to God and apply their minds to mental prayer, without leaving their occupations, their work, or who meditate even while traveling. He who seeks God will find Him, everywhere and at all times.

ST. ALPHONSUS LIGUORI

There are more tears shed over answered prayers than over unanswered prayers.

ST. THÉRÈSE OF LISIEUX

The whole aim of whoever intends to give himself to prayer ought to be to labor, to resolve, to dispose himself, with all possible diligence, to conform his will to that of God. For in this consists all the highest perfection that can be acquired in the spiritual way.

ST. TERESA OF ÁVILA

Prayer is the place of refuge for every worry, a foundation for cheerfulness, a source of constant happiness, a protection against sadness.

ST. JOHN CHRYSOSTOM

As our body cannot live without nourishment, so our soul cannot spiritually be kept alive without prayer.

ST. AUGUSTINE

We should have frequent recourse to prayer, and persevere a long time in it. God wishes to be solicited. He is not weary of hearing us.

ST. JOHN BAPTIST DE LA SALLE

Prayer ought to be humble, fervent, resigned, persevering, and accompanied with great reverence. One should consider that he stands in the presence of a God, and speaks with a Lord before whom the angels tremble from awe and fear.

ST. MARY MAGDALEN DE' PAZZI

There is a certain method of prayer which is both very easy and very useful. It consists in accustoming our soul to the presence of God in such a way to produce in us a union with Him which is intimate, simple, and perfect.

ST. FRANCIS DE SALES

The highest and most perfect prayer is contemplation. But this is altogether the work of God, as it is supernatural and above our powers. The soul can only prepare itself for this prayer, and can do nothing in it. The best preparation is to live humbly, and to give ourselves in earnest to the acquisition of virtues, and especially to fraternal charity and love of God; to have a firm resolution to do the will of God in all things; to walk in the way of the Cross, and to destroy self-love, which is a wish, on our part, to please ourselves rather than God.

ST. TERESA OF ÁVILA

These are questions I must put to you, for I have no one else to answer them.

ST. AUGUSTINE

The air which we breathe, the bread which we eat, the heart which throbs in our bosoms, are not more necessary for man that he may live as a human being, than is prayer for the Christian that he may live as a Christian.

ST. JOHN EUDES

It is simply impossible to lead, without the aid of prayer, a virtuous life.

ST. JOHN CHRYSOSTOM

No one can approach God without withdrawing from the world. By withdrawal I do not mean change of physical dwelling place, but withdrawal from worldly affairs. The virtue of withdrawal from the world consists in not occupying your mind with the world. If a man reads lines of great meaning without going deeply into them, his heart remains poor; and the holy force which, through wondrous understanding of the soul, gives most sweet food to the heart, grows dim in him. Prayer is one thing, and contemplation in prayer is another . . . Prayer is sowing; contemplation the reaping of the harvest, when the reaper is filled with wonder at the ineffable sight of the beautiful ears of corn, which have sprung before him from the little naked seeds that he sowed.

ST. ISAAC OF SYRIA

Mental prayer consists in weighing and understanding what we are saying, who it is to whom we are speaking and who we are to have the courage to speak to so great a Lord. To have these and similar thoughts is properly to make mental prayer.

ST. TERESA OF ÁVILA

Do not distress yourself about your prayers.
It is not always necessary to employ words,
even inwardly, it is enough to raise your heart
and let it rest in our Lord,
to look lovingly up toward this divine Lover
of our souls for between lovers
the eyes speak more eloquently than the tongue.

ST. FRANCIS DE SALES

It is by the spirit of prayer that the moral man is formed, for life is an internal movement. Our being is not constructed from without like a clay model; it develops from within, as a tree grows and blossoms with the rising of the sap. In us, the sap is the Spirit of Christ. Prayer stimulates its rise.

FR. ANTOINE SERTILLANGES, O.P.

To judge rightly of the goodness
and perfection of anyone's prayer,
it is sufficient to know the disposition
he takes to it, and the fruits he reaps from it.

ST. VINCENT DE PAUL

The power of prayer is really tremendous.

ST. THÉRÈSE OF LISIEUX

Conversation with God takes place in the depths and core of the soul. It is there that the soul speaks to God heart to heart, and always in a deep and profound peace that the soul enjoys in God. Everything that takes place outside the soul means no more to it than a lit straw that goes out as soon as it is ignited; it almost never, or very rarely, disturbs its inner peace.

BROTHER LAWRENCE

The whole aim of any person who is beginning prayer—and don't forget this, because it's very important—should be that he work and prepare himself with determination and every possible effort to bring his will into conformity with God's will . . . It is the person who lives in more perfect conformity who will receive more from the Lord and be more advanced on this road.

ST. TERESA OF ÁVILA

True, whole prayer is nothing but love.

ST. AUGUSTINE

Prayer is the inner bath of love into which the soul plunges itself.

ST. JOHN VIANNEY

God has instituted prayer so as to confer upon his creatures the dignity of being causes.

BLAISE PASCAL

⊡

We ascend to the heights of contemplation by the steps of the active life.

POPE ST. GREGORY I THE GREAT

◉

Remember . . . to retire occasionally into the solitude of your heart while you are outwardly engaged in business or conversation . . . Withdraw, then, your thoughts, from time to time, into your heart, where, separated from all men, you may familiarly treat with God on the affairs of your souls.

ST. FRANCIS DE SALES

⊡

If, while one is praying, he regards and considers the fact that he is conversing with God with more attention than the words that he utters, he is making vocal and mental prayer at once, which may be of much advantage to him. But if he does not consider with whom he is speaking, nor what he is saying, it may be thought certain that, however much he may move his lips, he prays very little.

ST. TERESA OF ÁVILA

Prayer is a ladder leading up to God; for there is nothing more powerful than prayer. There is no sin which cannot be forgiven by means of prayers, and there is no sentence of punishment which it cannot undo. There is no revelation which does not have prayer as its cause, and there are no types of symbols which prayer cannot interpret.

ANONYMOUS

Set my heart on the Kingdom? Fine, but how does one do this? . . . One simple answer is to move from the mind to the heart by slowly saying a prayer with as much attentiveness as possible.

HENRI NOUWEN

One way to begin prayer is to return ourselves to the present moment, and then to focus our attention on God in that moment. Begin by focusing your attention on your breathing. Give it your full attention. Breathe in slowly, then breathe out slowly. Do this for a minimum of three breaths, or for as long as it takes for your inner self to become calm and to give up any thoughts or images. If it helps, you can even say in your mind what you are doing, such as "breathe in one, breathe out one, breathe in two, breathe out two . . ."

ST. FRANCIS DE SALES

You wrote to me: "To pray is to talk with God. But about what?" About what? About him, and yourself: joys, sorrows, successes and failures, great ambitions, daily worries—even your weaknesses! And acts of thanksgiving and petitions—and love and reparation. In short, to get to know him and to get to know yourself—"to get acquainted!"

ST. JOSEMARÍA ESCRIVÁ

Much more is accomplished by a single word of the Our Father said, now and then, from our heart, than by the whole prayer repeated many times in haste and without attention.

ST. TERESA OF ÁVILA

At the times when you remember God, increase your prayers, so that when you forget Him, the Lord may remind you.

ST. MARK THE ASCETIC

TEN

Joy

THE BLESSING OF BEING ALIVE

◫

Happiness of mind and heart in serving God
—THE BALTIMORE CATECHISM

We all know the delicious feeling of being one with the world, of having a full heart torn between laughter and tears—that sense of deep appreciation for all that we behold, and high emotion that we are so at peace with our world.

It is a feeling we all strive for, sometimes against the odds. We try not to let our troubles make us forget the miracle of which we are a part, try not to stop noticing the myriad things to give us gladness wherever we turn. Some days it all just fits together and makes sense. Other days it doesn't.

The secret to perennial joy may lie in appreciating and cherishing the bad moments as well as the good, in accepting with tranquility the fact that life is not always roses and chocolate. There is no living without obstacles to surmount and strife in some area of our lives. It is the reality of the human condition.

When things are difficult, it's not because something is wrong with us or the world; it's because life is like that. Good and evil, happiness and sadness, sickness and health are all part of the package. It helps to stop struggling against it and try to accept with equanimity whatever life throws our way and remain contented with the treasures we have been given. The light of our sublime joy in being a part of creation, with a beautiful world to live in and people to love and be loved by, can outshine the darkness around us.

Anyone who tries to describe the ineffable Light in language is truly a liar—not because he hates the truth, but because of the inadequacy of his description.

ST. GREGORY OF NYSSA

We could talk and laugh together and exchange small acts of kindness. We could join in the pleasure that books can give. We could be grave or gay together. If we sometimes disagreed, it was without spite, as a man might differ with himself, and the rare occasions of dispute were the very spice to season our usual accord. Each of us had something to learn from the others and something to teach in return. If any were away, we missed them with regret and gladly welcomed them when they came home. Such things as these are heartfelt tokens of affection between friends. They are signs to be read on the face and in the eyes, spoken by the tongue and displayed in countless acts of kindness. They can kindle a blaze to melt our hearts and weld them into one.

ST. AUGUSTINE

With all things, it is always what comes to us from outside, freely and by surprise as a gift from heaven, without our having sought it, that brings us pure joy.

SIMONE WEIL

With God, nothing is empty of meaning.

ST. IRENAEUS

Every moment of each day I have the chance to choose between cynicism and joy. Every thought I have can be cynical or joyful. Every word I speak can be cynical or joyful. Every action can be cynical or joyful. Increasingly, I am aware of all these possible choices, and increasingly I discover that every choice for joy in turn reveals more joy and offers more reason to make life a true celebration in the house of the Father.

HENRI NOUWEN

Joy is the most infallible sign of the presence of God.

PIERRE TEILHARD DE CHARDIN

Spiritual joy arises from purity of the heart and perseverance in prayer.

ST. FRANCIS OF ASSISI

I travel, I work, suffer my weak health, meet with a thousand difficulties, but all these are nothing, for this world is so small. To me, space is an imperceptible object, as I am accustomed to dwell in eternity.

ST. FRANCES CABRINI

Little things seem nothing, but they give peace, like those meadow flowers which individually seem odorless but all together perfume the air.

GEORGES BERNANOS

Happy the man whose words issue from the Holy Spirit and not from himself.

ST. ANTHONY OF PADUA

Those who are led by the Holy Spirit have true ideas; that is why so many ignorant people are wiser than the learned. The Holy Spirit is light and strength.

ST. JOHN VIANNEY

Keep God's word in this way. Let it enter into your very being, let it take possession of your desires and your whole way of life. Feed on goodness, and your soul will delight in its richness.

ST. BERNARD OF CLAIRVAUX

It is so beautiful to count on God for everything!

BLESSED JEANNE JUGAN

Is it not true that when we have God we have everything?

ST. PETER JULIAN EYMARD

Who except God can give you peace? Has the world ever been able to satisfy the heart?

ST. GERARD MAJELLA

How can he abide long in peace who thrusts himself into the cares of others, who seeks occasions abroad, who little or seldom concentrates his own thought? Blessed are the single-hearted: for they shall have much peace.

THOMAS À KEMPIS

How is it, then, that I seek you, Lord? Since in seeking you, my God, I seek a happy life, let me seek you so that my soul may live, for my body draws life from my soul and my soul draws life from you.

ST. AUGUSTINE

From my infancy until now, in the seventieth year of my age, my soul always beheld this sight . . . The brightness which I see is not limited by space and is more brilliant than the radiance around the Sun . . . Sometimes when I see it, all sadness and pain is lifted from me, and I seem a simple girl again, and an old woman no more.

ST. HILDEGARD VON BINGEN

God has infinite treasure to bestow. When He finds a soul penetrated with a lively faith, He pours into it His graces and favors plentifully. There they flow like a torrent, spreading with impetu-osity and abundance.

BROTHER LAWRENCE

In anything at all, perfection is finally attained not when there is no longer anything to add, but when there is no longer anything to take away.

ANTOINE DE ST.-EXUPÉRY

. . . even as a child I existed, I was alive, I had the power of feel-ing; I had an instinct to keep myself safe and sound, to preserve my own being, which was a trace of the single unseen Being from whom it was derived. . . . Should I not be grateful that so small a creature possessed such wonderful qualities? But they were all gifts from God, for I did not give them to myself. His gifts are good and the sum of them all is my own self. Therefore, the God who made me must be good and all the good in me is his.

ST. AUGUSTINE

Without work, it is impossible to have fun.

ST. THOMAS AQUINAS

Our nature imposes on us a certain pattern of development which we must follow if we are to fulfill our best capacities and achieve at least the partial happiness of being human. This pattern must be properly understood and it must be worked out in all its essential elements. Otherwise, we fail. But it can be stated very simply, in a single sentence: *We must know the truth, and we must love the truth we know, and we must act according to the measure of our love.*

THOMAS MERTON

When we are at peace, we find the freedom to be most fully who we are, even in the worst of times. We let go of what is nonessential and embrace what is essential. We empty ourselves so that God may more fully work within us. And we become instruments in the hands of the Lord.

JOSEPH CARDINAL BERNARDIN

The farther you withdraw from earthly things,
The closer you approach heavenly things,
The more you find God.

ST. JOHN OF THE CROSS

God is closer to us than water is to a fish.

ST. CATHERINE OF SIENA

Blessed are they who crave sanctity, for their desire shall be fulfilled.

ST. VINCENT PALLOTTI

Indeed, man wishes to be happy even when he so lives as to make happiness impossible.

ST. AUGUSTINE

The gate of heaven is very low; only the humble can enter it.

ST. ELIZABETH SETON

The whole science of the saints consists in knowing and following the will of God.

ST. ISIDORE OF SEVILLE

If man is not made for God, why is he happy only in God? If man is made for God, why is he opposed to God?

BLAISE PASCAL

I found Him when I took leave of all creatures. I found Him in my inmost heart. When I am silent with men I am able to converse with God and with Him I always find perfect peace.

So abandon yourself utterly for the love of God, and in this way, you will become truly happy.

BLESSED HENRY SUSO

I found Him when I took leave of all creatures. I found Him in my inmost heart. When I am silent with men I am able to converse with God and with Him I always find perfect peace.

BROTHER LAWRENCE

God loves each of us as if there were only one of us.

ST. AUGUSTINE

Epigraph

Trust the Church of God implicitly even when your natural judgment would take a different course from hers and would induce you to question her prudence or correctness. Recollect what a hard task she has; how she is sure to be criticized and spoken against, whatever she does; recollect how much she needs your loyal and tender devotion; recollect, too, how long is the experience gained over so many centuries, and what a right she has to claim your assent to principles which have had so extended and triumphant a trial. Thank her that she has kept the faith safe for so many generations and do your part in helping her to transmit it to generations after you . . . O long sought-after desire of the eyes, joy of the heart, the truth after many shadows, the fullness after many foretastes, the home after many storms—come to her, poor wanderers, for she it is, and she alone, who can unfold the meaning of your being and the secret of your destiny.

—John Henry Cardinal Newman

Biographical Sketches

St. Aloysius Gonzaga (1568–1591) The patron saint of Catholic youth, Aloysius was a young Italian nobleman who received his first communion from the famed St. Charles Borromeo. He renounced his vast inheritance and joined the Society of Jesus, the Jesuits, dying at the age of twenty-three while caring for the stricken in Rome during an outbreak of plague. His simple wisdom earned his lasting fame, and he is a valuable inspiration for young people.

St. Alphonsus Liguori (1696–1787) A moral theologian and founder of the Redemptorists, Alphonsus was a beloved preacher who was at his very best in front of the most uneducated audiences. He once declared that he had never given a sermon that could not be appreciated by the most humble old woman in the crowd. At the same time, he crafted a detailed and rich moral system that is renowned for its subtlety.

St. Angela Merici (1474–1540) The foundress of the Ursulines, Angela spent her early years as a Franciscan tertiary, working for some time to care for the sick women of Brescia and to educate young girls. In 1524–1525, she went on a pilgrimage to the Holy Land, but while there, she was stricken temporarily with blindness. After recovering her sight, she pledged herself to God and founded the Order of the Ursulines in Brescia in 1535. The Ursulines became the oldest teaching order of women in the Church. Angela was canonized in 1807.

St. Anselm of Canterbury (c. 1033–1109) The archbishop of Canterbury, Anselm is considered one of the fathers of the Scholastic movement, the long-ranging union of philosophy and theology that dominated in the Church until the twentieth century. He is perhaps best known for creating an ontological argument for the existence of God using a simple notion that the existence of the Creator proves his being. He coined the term *Credo ut intelligam* ("I believe in order to understand").

St. Anthony of Padua (1195–1231) A Franciscan friar and Doctor of the Church, Anthony was a renowned preacher who gave up all his offices and positions in 1230 to devote himself to preaching. He concentrated himself in the area around Padua, routinely attracting enormous crowds of faithful who gathered eagerly to hear his words. While at Padua, he reportedly performed a miracle by restoring a severed foot. Retiring to Camposanpiere, near Padua, he fell ill in 1231, dying at Vercelli on June 13. A great patron of the poor, he is also invoked as protection for travelers, pregnant women, and lost property.

St. Anthony of the Desert (251–356) Also known as Antony of Egypt, he is honored as the father of all monks and the founder of Christian monasticism. Born in Egypt, he gave up all thought of a normal life and instead gave himself to a life of staggering austerity. He ate only bread and water, lived for a time in a cemetery tomb near his native village, and was said to have been tested by the devil and his demons, who appeared in the disguise of wild animals. Not surprisingly, St. Anthony is the central character in a host of different legends.

St. Augustine (354–430) The greatest of the Fathers of the Western Church and a saint who exercised an enormous influence on the formation of Christian theology and Western civilization, Augustine is a model for anyone making the journey from doubt to faith. He pursued God in philosophy, among the heretical Manichaeans, Neoplatonism, and finally in Christianity. Augustine finally found what he had been seeking, writing, *Inquietum cor nostrum est, donec requiescat in te* ("Our hearts are restless until they rest in You"). Once baptized into the faith, he emerged as one of the most remarkable theologians and Christian philosophers. His writings included 113 books, 218 letters, and some 500 sermons. Of these, his most famous books were *City of God* and *Confessions*. *Confessions* is required reading for spiritual seekers, especially in its unflinching personal honesty.

St. Barsanuphius (d. c. 550) Hermit of Gaza, in Israel, and an Egyptian, Barsanuphius maintained his hermitage near a monastery in Gaza. He was famed in his day for taking a vow of silence, spending most of his life without uttering a word. He communicated only in writing. He was also famous for existing without food or water for long stretches of time in order to tame the flesh.

St. Basil (c. 329–379) Bishop of Caesarea and one of the foremost Doctors of the Church who was noted, with St. Athanasius, as a great defender of Christian orthodoxy against Arianism, with his brother St. Gregory of Nyssa and St. Gregory of Nazianzus, Basil is one of "The Three Cappadocians" who distinguished themselves in Church history. He is best known for his letters—366 in all— that not only reveal a remarkably holy and eloquent person, but are also full of practical advice for living as well.

Venerable Bede (673–735) Known popularly as the Venerable Bede (because of the great respect paid to him and his writings), he was an Anglo-Saxon historian, biblical scholar, and one of the greatest of all chroniclers of the Middle Ages. Most of what is known about his life comes to us from Bede himself, writing in the last chapter of *Historia Ecclesiastica* (Ecclesiastical History). Of Bede, the disciple Cuthbert declared: "I can truly declare that I never beheld with my eyes or heard with my ears anyone return thanks so unceasingly to the living God."

Hilaire Belloc (1870–1953) A poet, essayist, and historian, Belloc was a friend of G. K. Chesterton and, despite being born in France, a member of the British Parliament. Belloc was never a shy writer, and he joined G. K. Chesterton and his brother Cecil Chesterton in a number of political attacks, known as Chesterbellocs. Belloc used a powerful and often acerbic wit to drive home his arguments, and no one ever accused him of being understated in his defense of Catholicism. He should be read by anyone interested in being armed with intellectual weapons to defend Catholicism.

Pope Benedict XV (1854–1922) Pope from 1914–1922, Benedict and his reign were overshadowed by World War I (1914–1918). Throughout the war, he adopted a policy of impartiality, working to mediate a peace and bringing aid to the millions who were suffering. Because of the neutral stand of the Holy See, Benedict was punished by the victorious powers by being excluded from the peace negotiations at Versailles. Benedict himself was a quiet and very prayerful pontiff, in contrast to the strong personality of his successor, Pope Pius XI (1922–1939). He also set up an international missing persons bureau for contacts between prisoners and their families but was forced to close it because of the suspicion of warring nations that it was a front for espionage operations.

Georges Bernanos (1888–1948) A French novelist and polemicist, Bernanos was considered one of the foremost Catholic writers of his time. Devoutly Catholic, he was a dedicated critic of materialist culture and the excesses of Francisco Franco in Spain as well as a promoter of authentic Catholic culture for France. He authored several renowned novels, including *The Star of Satan* (1926, tr. 1940), *The Diary of a Country Priest* (1936, tr. 1937), and *Dialogue des Carmelites* (1949; adapted for the stage in 1952), each dealing with important themes of faith and spirituality. In 1938, he abandoned hope for France after the Munich pact with Hitler, migrating to Brazil where he remained throughout World War II.

St. Bernard of Clairvaux (1090–1153) The abbot of Clairvaux, mystic, and an important figure in the history of the medieval Church, Bernard entered the religious life at the age of twenty-three, embarking upon a life of rigorous austerity by declaring, "I was conscious of the need of my weak nature for strong medicine." In 1115, Bernard established a monastery at Clairvaux, and it became a center for the Cistercian order and gained for Bernard widespread fame as a brilliant abbot and deeply respected mystic whose guidance was sought by many in the Church and secular governments. His austerities were so severe, however, that his health was shattered. He took to living away from the main community at Clairvaux because the other monks could not bear to look at his emaciated face and body. Nevertheless, he is honored as a major figure in fostering the spiritual life. Among his many notable works were *De Diligendo Deo* (*On the Diligence of God*) and a beautiful sermon, "On the Song of Songs."

Joseph Cardinal Bernardin (1928–1996) The archbishop of Chicago and a cardinal, Joseph Bernardin earned lasting respect for the grace with which he faced his death from cancer. Ordained in 1952, Bernardin was named the archbishop of Cincinnati in 1972, archbishop of Chicago in 1982, and a cardinal in 1983. He proved himself a deeply pastoral archbishop, displaying immense fortitude and forbearance when falsely accused of molesting a young seminarian. The charge was disproved, but Bernardin suffered enormous humiliation, publicly forgiving his accuser. Soon after, he was diagnosed with terminal cancer. He subsequently published an account of his final days in the book *The Gift of Peace,* a moving journal of going to God with love, hope, and tranquility.

St. Birgitta of Sweden (c. 1303–1373) Also Brigitta and Birgida, a mystic, founder of the Brigittine order, and the patron saint of Sweden, Birgitta was the mother of eight children, including St. Catherine of Sweden. After the death of her husband in 1344, she entered the religious life near the Cistercian monastery of Alvastra, on Lake Netter. There she dictated her numerous visions and divine messages. She was later one of the most well-traveled women in Christendom, and her pilgrimages included Rome and Jerusalem. Throughout her life, she offered useful advice to her fellow sisters on how to advance toward spiritual perfection and the life of prayer.

Boethius (c. 480–c. 524) A Roman statesman and intellectual, Boethius was one of the last great philosophers of the Roman tradition and a brilliant thinker in an age marked by barbarian invasions and social chaos. Boethius wrote his most famous work, *De Consolatione Philosophiae* (*The Consolation of Philosophy*), while awaiting execution in prison after offending the ruler of the Ostrogoths. In the work, Boethius argued that knowledge of virtue and God were attainable by the study of philosophy.

Mother Cabrini (1850–1917) Italian foundress and the first American citizen to be canonized, Mother Cabrini, in 1880, founded the Missionary Sisters of the Sacred Heart, a community of religious women that expanded to the United States at the urging of Pope Leo XIII. Cabrini arrived in New York on March 31, 1889, and embarked upon the care of Italian immigrants. Her work took her to slums, hospitals, and prisons, and she established schools, orphanages, and care centers. She sailed back and forth across the ocean to Europe some thirty times, laboring with her sisters throughout the United States (and then South America and Europe), including New York, Denver, Los Angeles, Chicago, Philadelphia, and Seattle. Her travels were made even more remarkable by the fact that she had a terrible fear of water owing to a childhood accident. She became a naturalized American citizen in 1909 and died in Chicago in 1917. Canonized in 1946 by Pope Pius XII, she was named in 1950 the patroness of all emigrants. Her spirituality has come to be appreciated in recent years.

St. Catherine of Genoa (1447–1510) An Italian mystic, Catherine was the daughter of a noble family and spent the early years of her married life with a dissolute and wayward husband who drove them into financial ruin. With her encouragement, he reformed his life and became a Third Order Franciscan. Catherine, meanwhile, became known for her work in the hospitals and poor sections of Genoa, not to mention as a gifted mystic. She wrote *Dialogue Between the Soul and the Body* and *Treatise on Purgatory,* both revered as outstanding books on mysticism.

St. Catherine Labouré (d. 1876) A French mystic, Catherine received a vision of the Miraculous Medal. After joining the Sisters of Charity of St. Vincent de Paul in 1830, Catherine was sent to the convent at Paris. There she received visions of Our Lady in the chapel, and she was asked by the Blessed Virgin to strike a medal depicting the Virgin and honoring the Immaculate Conception. From very humble beginnings, the medal became so immensely popular that it earned the title "Miraculous." Catherine spent the rest of her life working in a hospital.

St. Catherine of Siena (1347–1380) One of the greatest medieval mystics and the patron saint of Italy, Catherine was also a Doctor of the Church, a Dominican, and an adviser to several popes. Catherine was the youngest of twenty-five children and received her first mystical experience at age six. Revered for her holiness and abilities as a peacemaker and counselor, she actually convinced Pope Gregory XI (r. 1370–1378) to return the papacy to Rome from France for the first time in nearly a century and made peace among several Italian cities. A profound mystic, she practiced such severe austerities that they hastened her death.

Teilhard de Chardin, Pierre (1881–1955) A French Jesuit theologian and scientist, de Chardin is both a controversial and eloquent author whose works included both theological and spiritual efforts. At his death, however, only his scientific papers had been published, and his body of theological and spiritual books long remained unpublished. These were eventually published and widely read, although de Chardin never intended to write theological treatises. His books include (*The Divine Milieu*; written in 1927, published in 1957), an effort to express his own religious experience, and (*The Phenomenon of Man*, 1955), expressing his positive view of the universe, which he saw as an ongoing evolutionary process of movement toward systems of increasing complexity. For de Chardin, all evolution is pointed toward a final, eschatological point, called the *divinus terminus*, or Omega Point, in which the universe is gathered into God. Since the Incarnation, this movement has been part of the "Christification" of the universe. Everything de Chardin wrote in terms of spirituality was colored by this insight.

Venerable Charles de Foucauld (1858–1916) A French missionary and martyr, Charles Eugene was the viscount de Foucauld and, thus, a French nobleman. He served as a French army officer in Algieria beginning in 1881 and commanded an expedition to map the various oases of Morocco in 1883. Three years later, he underwent a powerful conversion, and in 1890, he joined a Trappist monastery. The community life did not permit him to pray as he felt called to do, so he departed to become a hermit in Palestine. In 1901, he went back to Algeria; there he settled at Tamanrasset and labored as a missionary priest. Although acknowledged by all for his holiness, his efforts to preach the Gospel were opposed by some Islamic leaders, especially because they feared he might create a positive feeling toward the French colonial government. De Foucauld was, thus, murdered during an anti-French attack. His life and spirituality nevertheless encouraged men and women to follow his example, and in the 1930, his followers formed the Little Brothers of Jesus and the Little Sisters of Jesus to preach in Algeria in the same spirit as Charles.

G. K. Chesterton (1874–1936) One of the foremost English essayists and authors and a prominent convert to Catholicism in 1922, Chesterton wrote a host of famed books, including *The Catholic Church and Conversion* (1926), *The Everlasting Man* (1925), *Avowals and Denials* (1934), biographies of St. Francis of Assisi (1923) and St. Thomas Aquinas (1933), and his *Autobiography* (1936). Chesterton also authored the beloved detective series featuring Father Brown, the priest-sleuth who debuted in *The Innocence of Father Brown* in 1911. In 1936, Pope Pius XI granted him the remarkable title of "Defender of the Catholic Faith." Chesterton is required reading for contemporary believers seeking to find the fundamentals of belief written in a manner that is eminently logical, civilized, and delightfully sensible.

St. Clare of Assisi (1194–1253) A dear friend of St. Francis of Assisi and foundress of the Poor Clares, in 1212, Clare gave up all her possessions to join Francis on his remarkable spiritual journey. Clare was soon joined by many other women, including her sisters Agnes and Beatrice and eventually even her own widowed mother. Through her work, the Second Order of St. Francis was established. Clare was also declared in 1958 the patroness of television because she is known for her visions, including miraculously seeing and hearing the Christmas Mass taking place in the basilica on the opposite side of Assisi. Her spirituality was similar to that of Francis, stressing the gifts of simplicity and trusting completely in God.

Blessed Claude de la Colombierè (d. 1682) Jesuit preacher and missionary to England, de la Colombierè was sent to England in 1676 as chaplain to Mary Beatrice d'Este, the duchess of York. Much feared by the English because of his skills as a preacher, he was falsely accused in the Titus Oates plot to assassinate King Charles II (r. 1625–1649) and was banished after several difficult months in prison. His writings are noteworthy for stressing patience in the face of adversity.

Paul Claudel (1868–1955) A French poet, playwright, and essayist, Claudel wrote brilliant plays rich in Christian symbolism. These included *La Ville* (1893), *Le repos du septième jour* (1896), and

L'Annonce faite à Marie (1912). Other notable works included *Le Soulier de satin* (1924), *L'Otage* (1911), and *Le Père humilié* (1916).

St. Clement I (d. c. 97) Also called Clement of Rome, he was the third successor to St. Peter as Bishop of Rome. According to custom, Clement was a onetime slave in the household of Titus Flavius Clemens, the cousin of a Roman emperor. Other stories attest to his banishment to Crimea and martyrdom by having an anchor tied around his neck and then being thrown into the sea. Clement was most likely the author of the famed First Epistle of Clement, considered the most important Church document, outside of the NT and the *Didache,* of the first century. It is valuable reading for those interested in belonging to a community of believers.

St. Clement XI (d. 1721) Pope from 1700–1721, Clement is reputed to be one of the most learned and brilliant pontiffs in the history of the Church. He needed all of his intelligence, as he served as pope during one of the most difficult centuries in Church history.

St. Cyprian (d. 258) Bishop of Carthage and an important early Christian theologian, Cyprian was renowned for his wisdom and his skills as a writer. His correspondences, providing a clear picture of the times and the horrors of the Roman persecutions, consist of eighty-one items—sixty-five from Cyprian and sixteen in response to him from others. He also wrote *De Catholicae Ecclesiae Unitate* (or simply *De Unitate*), discussing the nature of unity in the Church and the ideal of equality among the bishops; *De Lapsis,* detailing the conditions by which the lapsed could be readmitted into the Church;

and *Ad Quirinam* (or *Testimonia*), a compilation of biblical proof texts. His most famous maxim is "You cannot have God for your Father, if you cannot have the Church for your mother."

St. Cyril of Jerusalem (c. 315–386) Bishop of Jerusalem who was exiled from his diocese during the era of the Arian heresy, Cyril is also remembered for his ability to encourage moral reform and for being a great teacher of the faith. His primary surviving work is the *Catecheses,* eighteen instructional addresses for baptismal candidates during Lent and five for the newly baptized after Easter. The last five are known as the *Mystagogic,* as they are concerned with mysteries. His style is that of a loving father, and one should read him to understand the sacrament of baptism.

Leonardo da Vinci (1492–1519) An Italian inventor, sculptor, engineer, architect, and painter, Leonardo is considered one of the greatest geniuses of human history. Among his greatest works were *The Last Supper* (1495–1497) and the *Mona Lisa* (1503–1506). Aside from his works of art and feats of engineering, Leonardo was also a true visionary; his notebooks were filled with scientific insights centuries ahead of his time.

Dorothy Day (1879–1980) A social activist and founder of the Catholic Worker Movement, Dorothy Day sought to unite in her daily life her deep faith and her radical commitment to social justice. Always drawn to social justice issues, she gradually made her way to Catholicism, seeing it as "the church of immigrants, the church of the poor." Baptized a Catholic in 1927, she grounded her decades of activism in Catholic social teaching, founding *The*

Catholic Worker with Peter Maurin and the Catholic Worker Movement. The movement spread across the United States in the 1930s and was a vocal opponent of the U.S. involvement in World War II, Korea, and Vietnam. Day also supported the civil rights movement and was jailed repeatedly for her positions against war and injustice.

Aside from her efforts on behalf of the poor and peace, she is a model for anyone seeking to rebuild their life after shattering personal experiences. In Day's case, the transforming event was an abortion. For the rest of her life, she committed herself to God and to prayer, once declaring, "If I have achieved anything in my life, it is because I have not been embarrassed to talk about God." She was very demanding of herself and especially her friends, but she was also a strong voice for the human conscience and for raising our voices in defense of the poor and the helpless.

Catherine Doherty (1896–1985) The founder of the Madonna House and social activist, Catherine was a friend of Dorothy Day and Thomas Merton. Born in Russia to a Russian Orthodox family, she converted to the Catholic Church in 1920. With her then husband, Boris de Hueck, she barely survived the Russian Revolution, escaping finally to Canada and New York, where Catherine worked as a laundress, maid, sales clerk, and waitress. Eventually, she became a lecturer and an advocate for the poor and for social justice, authoring hundreds of magazine articles and more than thirty books, including *Poustinia,* a classic of modern spirituality. In 1947, Catherine and her second husband, Eddie Doherty, founded the Madonna House, a community of laypeople and priests who labor to live out the Gospel in their daily lives.

St. Dominic (c. 1170–1221) The founder of the Order of the Friars Preachers, the Dominicans, and one of the most important spiritual leaders of the Middle Ages, Dominic ranks with St. Francis as one of the great inspirations for reform and for combining the life of prayer and the life of work in the world. The order he created eventually won official recognition in 1216 and claimed such remarkable members as St. Thomas Aquinas. St. Dominic is also credited with developing the great Catholic tradition of the rosary.

St. Katherine Drexel (1858–1955) An American heiress, Katherine devoted her fortune to the care and education of Native Americans and African Americans in an era when few people were concerned about either. She founded the Sisters of the Blessed Sacrament for Indians and Colored People. Under Katherine's leadership, the sisters established St. Catherine's School for Pueblo Indians (in Santa Fe, New Mexico, in 1894), followed by other schools and missions. In 1915, she and the order launched Xavier University in New Orleans, which at the time was the only such institution in the United States devoted to the education of African Americans. She was declared a saint in 2001.

Meister Eckhart (c. 1260–c. 1328) A Medieval German mystic, Eckhart was given the title *magister sacrae theologiae* (master of sacred theology) from which his name, Meister, was derived in honor of his staggering knowledge of theology. Ironically, his speculative theology made him the first Dominican to be accused of heresy. His complex writings reveal a tendency toward a kind of pantheism, calling for personal prayer and *Gottesgeburt in der Seele* (the birth of God in the soul), bringing with it the overcoming of temporal concerns and the reflecting of the divine light of God. He authored fifty-nine known sermons (he was a brilliant preacher) and numerous works in German: *Buch der göttlichen Trösting* (*Book of Divine Consolation*); *Von Aberscheidenheit* (*On Emptiness*); *Reden der Unterscheidung* (*Talks of Instruction*); and *Rechtfertigungschrift* (*Letter of Justification*), a defense of his own works. He influenced such notable mystics as Henry Suso and Johannes Tauler.

St. Elizabeth Ann Seton (1774–1821) The first American-born saint and founder and first superior of the Sisters of Charity, she was born in New York and was the daughter of non-Catholics. She entered the Church on March 14, 1805, to the consternation of her Anglican family. Over the next years, she faced such anti-Catholic hostility in New York that she migrated to Baltimore. There, in 1808, she opened a school next to the chapel of St. Mary's Seminary. She was soon joined by other women, and in June 1809, the little community was transferred to Emmitsburg to care for poor children. Mother Seton had thus founded a new religious community, and, against her will, Elizabeth was elected superior. All the sisters took their vows on July 19, 1813. They soon spread to other cities, but Mother Seton continued to work up in Emmitsburg until the time of her death on January 4, 1821. She was canonized by Pope Paul VI in 1975.

St. Eusebius of Caesarea (c. 260–340) The so-called Father of Church History, one of the most important of all Church historians and bishop of Caesarea, his ecclesiastical career was much helped by his friendship with Emperor Constantine the Great, to whom he delivered an honorific speech in 335 and composed a panegyric at his death in 337, the *Vita Constantini* (*Life of Constantine*). A prolific writer, Eusebius was the author of the *Praeparatio Evangelica* (*Preparation for the Gospel*); *Demonstratio Evangelica* (*Demonstration of the Gospel*); *Chronicle* (covering from Abraham to Eusebius's own era, translated by St. Jerome from the Greek); *Theophany*, on the Incarnation; and *De Solemnitate Paschali* (on the Solemnity of Easter), a treatise on Easter. His most famous work was the *Historia Ecclesiastica* (*Ecclesiastical History*). Covering the events of the Church from its origins to 324, the history was poorly written with terrible Greek grammar, but it is a perfect glimpse into the long persecutions of the Church by the Roman Empire.

Evagrius Ponticus (346–399) One of the more important ascetical writers of his time, he was called Ponticus after Pontus, the place of his birth, a preacher of high repute in Constantinople. He left the imperial capital with its promise of high advancement in the Church. Instead, he departed the city for the Nitrian Desert and an ascetical life. His ascetical writings were later condemned by the Church, but there is no doubt about his personal holiness.

François de Salignac Fénelon (1651–1715) In full, François de Salignac de la Mothe-Fénelon, archbishop of Cambrai, was unusual for his time by opposing the often bitter treatment of Protestants in France, preferring to promote a peaceful process of convincing his hearers of the rightness of the Catholic faith. In 1695, he was made archbishop of Cambrai and was drawn subsequently to the mystical. Fénelon later wrote the controversial *Explication des maximes des saints sur la vie intérieure* (*Explanation of the*

Sayings of the Saints on the Interior Life, 1697), an effort to express his own views on the life of prayer. Pope Innocent XII condemned twenty-three propositions in the book, to which Fénelon submitted. He later wrote the *Traité sur l'existence de Dieu* (*Treatise on the Existence of God*; 1712, in part; 1731, complete).

St. Frances of Rome (1384–1440) Founder of the Oblate Congregation of Tor de'Specchi, Frances is considered the model for the ideal wife and widow. She wed in 1347, despite her private desire to join a religious order, and was a devoted wife. In 1425, with her husband's support, she founded a society of women to help the poor, the start of the Oblates. She served as their mother superior after her husband's passing. Frances was noted for being blessed by being able to see her guardian angel. She was also declared patron of motorists by Pope Pius XI.

St. Francis of Assisi (c. 1181–1226) Founder of the Franciscan order, Francis is one of the most famous and beloved of all saints. The story of Francis is one of the best known—the son of a wealthy cloth merchant, he gave up everything to follow Christ in poverty and service. His preaching and care for the poor earned him notoriety and the title *Il Poverello* (The Little Poor Man). Others joined him, some of the earliest and most notable being the merchant Bernard, the canon Pietro, and the famous Brother Giles (St. Giles of Assisi). For them and the others who gathered about him, Francis composed a simple rule of life, called the *regula primitiva*. This rule he took to Rome in 1210, where he won approval for it from Pope Innocent III (r. 1198–1216), whose initial reluctance was melted supposedly by a dream in which he saw Francis holding up the walls of St. John Lateran. So began the Franciscan order. Its members practiced rigorous asceticism and extreme poverty, relying upon alms as they wandered across Italy to preach. As for Francis, he journeyed to the Holy Land to preach among the Muslims and returned home to a life of intense prayer and holiness. He received the stigmata in 1224 and died after great suffering (including blindness). A saint of deceptive simplicity, Francis composed a number of hymns and prayers and possibly the famed "Canticle of the Sun."

St. Francis de Sales (1567–1622) One of the greatest spiritual writers in the history of the Church, Francis is honored as a Doctor of the Church and patron of the Catholic press. Passing up a brilliant political career, Francis entered the priesthood and was named the bishop of Geneva in 1602. He wasted no time reforming his diocese, preaching throughout every parish and acting as a tireless confessor. It is said that he was personally responsible for converting more than 50,000 Protestant to the Catholic faith. Francis is best known for his extremely popular devotional writings. Chief among these were the *Introduction to the Devout Life* (1609) and *Treatise on the Love of God* (1616). The *Introduction* began as a small, practical manual for use by his cousin's wife and was intended to encourage the life of prayer and devotion. It was much respected by a wide cross section of European culture, including King James I of England. One of his most important maxims declared "It is a mistake, a heresy, to want to exclude devoutness of life from among soldiers, from shops and offices, from royal courts, from the homes of the married." Francis is one of the best sources of inspiration for anyone hoping to achieve spiritual depth in the seemingly ordinary life. For Francis, anyone can master the virtues and reach the greatest perfection while fulfilling the demands of the modern world.

St. Francis Xavier (1506–1552) Spanish Jesuit and one of the greatest missionaries in the history of the Church, Francis's work in the Far East earned him the title "Apostle of the East Indies" and "Apostle of Japan." In the course of his truly vast missionary labors from 1542 to 1552, Francis visited most of Asia and was responsible for the conversion of thousands (Jesuit sources put the number at 700,000), leaving behind him organized and thriving Christian communities. His last expedition was to China, a land then forbidden to all foreigners. He landed on the island of Shangchwan and fell ill while waiting for a Chinese junk that was supposed to transport him in secret to the mainland. His hopes of entering China died with him in a small hut on Shangchwan. Francis is a model of Jesuit zeal and the willingness to give everything for a cause, even one's life.

St. Gaudentius of Brescia (d. c. 410) An Italian bishop, he was a friend and supporter of some of the greatest figures of his age, including St. Ambrose and St. John Chrysostom. Gaudentius, in fact, spent some time in prison for refusing to denounce John Chrysostom when the famed saint was under attack at the court of Emperor Arcadius (r. 395–408).

St. Gerard Majella (d. 1755) A Redemptorist lay brother, Gerard was a disciple of St. Alphonsus Liguori. A mystic with genuinely astounding gifts, Gerard was famed for his abilities at bilocation, as well as his prophecies, visions, and other spiritual phenomena. He died of consumption.

Luigi Giussani (1922–) An Italian priest, theologian, and founder of the Communion and Liberation movement, an association for lay people, and long concerned with education and the study of faith, Giussani taught in seminaries and high schools. The Communion and Liberation movement was begun in 1954 by Giussani in a high school in Milan with a group of young people. Its objective is to foster the Christian maturity of its members and collaboration in the mission of the Church in all areas of modern life. The movement is found in more than seventy countries.

Graham Greene (1901–1991) An English author and convert, Greene was one of the most successful novelists of the twentieth century, with such classic works as *Our Man in Havana*, *The Quiet American*, *The Third Man*, and *The Fallen Idol*. After a troubled youth as the son of a headmaster, he flirted with communism and eventually took a job at *The Times* in London. He gave up the post to devote himself to full-time novel writing. He met his future wife, Vivien Dayrell-Browning, when she wrote to correct several errors regarding Catholicism in his writings. At her urging, Greene was received into the Church in 1926. His 1940 novel, *The Power and the Glory*, was attacked by many Catholics for its portrayal of a whiskey priest.

Pope St. Gregory I the Great (d. 604) Pope from 590–604 and the last of the Latin Fathers of the Church, Gregory never wanted to be pope, but once elected, gave of himself absolutely.

He described his commitment to the Church by taking as his motto, *Servus servorum Dei* ("Servant of the Servants of God"). The welfare of even the poorest person was his concern, and he once wept openly to learn that someone had starved to death in Rome.

St. Gregory of Nyssa (c.335–395) Bishop of Nyssa, brother of St. Basil the Great, Gregory was one of the so-called Cappadocian Fathers (with Basil and Gregory of Nazianzus)—as they were all from the region of Cappadocia. Considered the leading theologian of his age, Gregory was also a voluminous writer, authoring treatises and a variety of works on spirituality, homilies, sermons, and letters. Two of his most readable works are "On Perfection" and "On Virginity." The former is especially useful for encouraging prayer and the cultivation of the virtues.

Romano Guardini (1885–1968) An Italian priest, theologian, and writer, Guardini is one of the most widely read Catholic authors in Europe. His long life and ministry stretched across two world wars, the Holocaust, and the massive changes that took place in the Church in the years after the Second Vatican Council. His writings encompassed spiritual and intellectual advice, as well as extensive insight into the liturgy and especially meditations on the person and the life of Jesus Christ. He is a valuable source for those seeking to understand how to believe in a modern world full of challenges to belief and hope. Among his notable works are *The Art of Praying: The Principles and Methods of Christian Prayer, The Lord,* and *The End of the Modern World.*

Guigo the Carthusian (1084–c. 1136) A Carthusian monk, Guigo was also a gifted ascetical writer and organizer of the method of praying the Lectio Divina (the Church ancient traditions of prayer). His other writings include various letters to the most famous figures of his age, including St. Bernard of Clairvaux and several popes. He was thus known to his contemporaries for his holiness and practical advice for advancing in the spiritual life. Of particular note is the *Scala Paradisi* (at least attributed to him), a guide for prayer and progress along the ladders of spirituality to paradise.

Madame Jeanne Guyon Marie Bouvier de la Mothe (1648–1717) A French mystic, Madame Guyon was one of the chief exponents of the spiritual movement called Quietism. The Quietists taught that true attainment required spiritual annihilation and the total absorption of the will by God. These teachings ran counter to Church teaching, and she was imprisoned by French authorities for many years. Her friend Archbishop François de Salignac Fénelon defended her, with little success.

Heloise (d. 1164) The doomed wife of the controversial theologian Abelard, Heloise was the niece of a canon of Notre Dame cathedral in Paris. Placed under the tutelage of Abelard, she soon fell in love with him, beginning one of the most tragic romances of the Middle Ages. The two were secretly married, and Heloise gave birth to a son, Astrolabe. When her uncle learned of the marriage, however, he had Abelard castrated. Heloise fled to Arenteuil and later died of a broken heart. Only in death were they reunited, for

Abelard was buried at Pere-Lachaise Cemetery in Paris, next to his lost beloved.

Blessed Henry Suso (c. 1295–1366) A German mystic, Henry was a student and friend of Meister Eckhart and a member of the spiritual society of the *Gottesfreunde* (Friends of God). He authored several works on prayer and spirituality, including *The Little Book Eternal Wisdom*, which was the most widely read manual of mysticism in the fourteenth and fifteenth centuries in all of Christendom. His book was eclipsed only by the even more popular *Imitation of Christ*.

St. Hilary (d. 468) Pope from 461–468 during one of the darkest periods in European history. The Roman Empire was beset by Germanic invasions, and the Church was troubled by numerous ecclesiastical disputes. At one point, a mob in Rome almost killed Hilary. He survived by fleeing Rome and briefly hiding for his life in the tomb of John the Evangelist in Ephesus.

St. Hildegard von Bingen (1098–1179) A German mystic and abbess, Hildegard was called the "Sibyl of the Rhine" because of her many visions and prophecies. She was also one of the most powerful women in Europe, serving as an abbess and trusted friend to St. Bernard of Clairvaux. Hildegard wrote hymns, scientific treatises, and, above all, the *Scivias*, a collection of visions that were approved by the Pope. Her hymns and visions have been immensely popular in recent years, and Hildegard is honored as a voice for women in Church history.

Walter Hilton (d. 1396) An English mystic and devotional writer, Walter is best known for his famed *Ladder of Perfection* (1494), a two-volume guide on spiritual attainment. The first book of its kind to appear in England, it remained popular throughout the fifteenth and sixteenth centuries. His other works include *Epistle to a Devout Man in Temporal Estate* (1494) and *The Song of Angels* (1521), an exposition on the Psalms. It is also thought by some scholars that Hilton might also have been the author of the first three books of the *Imitation of Christ,* generally attributed to Thomas à Kempis.

St. Ignatius of Antioch (c. 35–107) Bishop of Antioch and an important early martyr, Ignatius was arrested by Roman authorities and sent to Rome to be executed. While on his way to die, Ignatius began writing epistles (or letters) to the Christian communities of Ephesus, Magnesia, Tralles, Rome, Philadelphia, and Smyrna, and a farewell letter to Bishop Polycarp. His letters are a powerful testimony of faith, but they also give encouragement to anyone facing ordeals that seem insurmountable. As he wrote, "Let me follow the example of the suffering of my God." He was granted his wish, suffering death by being thrown to the wild animals of the Roman circus.

St. Ignatius Loyola (1491–1556) The founder of the Jesuits, the Society of Jesus, and a saint who best exemplifies the powerful process of spiritual exercises, Ignatius was originally a soldier, but after he was wounded in the leg in 1521 during the siege of Pamplona, he underwent a remarkable conversion. As a result of his considerable mystical and spiritual growth, he began work on his famed *Spiritual Exercises*. In 1534, in Paris, he and his closest friends took vows of poverty, chastity, and, if possible, a missionary pilgrimage to the Holy Land, with service to the Holy See. So was born the Society of Jesus, the Jesuits. The order became the bulwark of the Catholic Reformation, and the Jesuits for centuries were both feared and respected for their devotion to the Church and the papacy. Ignatius's grueling four-week series of Spiritual Exercises is a proven set of meditations that will lead to holiness, assisting the student of prayer in fostering a vocation that is unique to his or her own skills and personality.

Pope Innocent III (d. 1216) Pope from 1198–1216 and one of the most formidable pontiffs of the Middle Ages. Deeply concerned with the spiritual welfare of the Church and Christians, Innocent wished to avoid political entanglements, but his reign was filled with temporal crises, including the terrible Fourth Crusade in 1204. He also gave his support to the Franciscans and Dominicans, helping lay the groundwork for the remarkable achievements of those two religious orders.

St. Isaac of Syria (d. c. 700) A bishop and theologian, Isaac gave up his position of authority in the Syrian Church and retired to a monastery. There he concerned himself with mystical and ascetic writings, originally in Syriac but translated into Arabic, Greek, and Ethiopic. The influence of his writings can be seen in Christian mysticism in the West.

St. Isidore of Seville (c. 560–636) The archbishop of Seville and the last of the so-called Latin Fathers of the Church, Isidore was an outspoken advocate of tolerance and respect for the Jews (at a time when anti-Semitism was gaining strength in Europe). He also authored the *Origines,* an encyclopedia of religious knowledge, as well as a history of the world from Creation to A.D. 615.

St. Jane Frances de Chantal (1572–1641) The French foundress of the Order of the Visitation, St. Jane was a close friend of St. Francis de Sales. In 1607, she assisted Francis in founding a new religious order for young women and widows who longed for the religious life but who could not endure the rules of the more severe and rigorous ascetic orders. She gave her life to the care of the sick and poor and was described by St. Vincent de Paul as "one of the holiest people I have ever met on this earth." St. Jane is a testament that the spiritual life is for all, regardless of personal circumstances or weaknesses.

St. Jeanne d'Arc (c. 1412–1431) The Maid of Orléans, or *La Pucelle,* Joan of Arc is a patron saint of France. She emerged from absolute obscurity as a mere peasant girl to lead the armies of France to victory against the English at Orléans. Joan emerged as a military captain after hearing the voices of St. Michael, St. Margaret, and St. Catherine, who told her to save France. At first dismissed, she persisted in convincing French leaders of her sincerity, finally winning the support of the uncrowned King Charles VII of France. In the famous episode, she stupefied the disguised dauphin and soon after won the approval of theologians at Poitier. Named commander of the forces gathered to relieve the besieged city of Orléans, she put on white armor and led the French to a stunning victory. The breaking of the siege led to Charles's coronation at

Reims on July 17, 1429, and to the ultimate defeat of England in the Hundred Years' War (1337–1453). Soon after, she was captured by the Burgundians and sold to the English. Condemned by a sham tribunal, she was burned at the stake, dying with a prayer on her lips.

Blessed Marie Jeanne Jugan of the Cross (1792–1879) The cofoundress of the Little Sisters of the Poor, Blessed Marie of the Cross began her apostolate in 1837, when she and two companions, Françoise Albert and Virginie Tredaniel, dedicated themselves to the care of the aged, the abandoned, and the needy. Her work was so remarkable that she was eventually awarded medals from the French Academy and even the Freemasons for her work. By 1851, Blessed Marie had five houses and more than three hundred sisters. At her death there were 2,400 Little Sisters of the Poor. Toward the end of her life, she suffered cruelly at the hands of a priest who took away control of the congregation. He dismissed her as superior and forced her to live in total obscurity among her own sisters. She did not complain about this outrageous behavior, viewing all things as providing grace. She is, thus, a model for bearing injustice and hardships. Today, she is revered for her holiness, and the priest is nothing more than an unpleasant footnote.

St. Jerome (c. 342–420) A Doctor of the Church and biblical scholar, Jerome was one of the most ardent Christians of his age, noted for his fiery temper and his biting pen. One of the greatest scholars of the early Church, Jerome utilized his long and comprehensive education to make extremely important literary contributions to the faith. His chief work was the translation of the Bible from Hebrew into Latin, the famed Vulgate. He also wrote *De viris illustribus* (*Lives of the Illustrious Men,* 392), presenting the leading ecclesiastical writers of the previous years; numerous letters, sent to the most notable leaders of the time; and various controversial treatises. A spirited and at times intemperate figure, Jerome entered eagerly into the controversies facing the Church, using his wit as a cudgel to batter opponents. His spiritual advice is very straightforward, and he was never one to suffer fools gladly.

Pope John XXII (d. 1334) Pope from 1316–1334, the second pontiff to reside in Avignon rather than Rome, John was elected because he was thought sick and, thus, not likely to accomplish much. He soon surprised his electors with drive and energy. He reorganized the Curia, founded new dioceses, promoted learning, codified Church law, sponsored missionary work in Asia, and improved papal finances. John also issued the first major papal declaration on Church music. He also canonized Thomas Aquinas. Even as pope, he practiced a frugal and simple lifestyle.

Pope Blessed John XXIII (1881–1963) Pope from 1958–1963 and one of the most popular of all pontiffs, John is best known for launching Vatican Council II (1962–1965). Angelo Giuseppe Roncalli spent long years as a papal diplomat, including service as permanent observer for the Holy See at UNESCO (United Nations Educational, Scientific, and Cultural Organization). In 1953, he was made a cardinal and patriarch of Venice. While there, he was a very popular figure, known for his wit, cordiality, and approachable pastoral style. His election as pope came as a complete surprise, but even more shocking was his decision to call for the Second Vatican Council. Said by John to be an inspiration of the Holy Spirit, the council was intended by the pope to bring *aggiornamento* (renewal), a new vibrant presentation of the faith in the modern world. Beyond the council, he issued several notable encyclicals: *Ad Cathedram Petri* (1959), *Mater et Magistra* (1961), and *Pacem in Terris* (1963), which preached "universal peace in truth, justice, charity, and liberty." He thereby took the first steps toward a dialogue with the Soviet Union and began to reach out to the other Christian denominations and faiths. John was also legendary for his humor and peasant's common sense. His chief spiritual writing was *Autobiography of a Soul*. He died of cancer and was beatified in 2000 by Pope John Paul II.

St. John of Ávila (1500–1569) A Spanish mystic, John was one of the great reformers of his time in Spain. For his work, he was called the Apostle of Andalusia, renewing the Christian faith in the region by his fiery sermons and his spiritual advice. Among those he counseled were Sts. Teresa of Ávila, Francis Borgia, and Luis of Granada. As Teresa once remarked, reliable spiritual advisers were one in 10,000. John must have been remarkable indeed.

St. John Baptist de la Salle (1651–1719) The founder of the Institute of the Brothers of Christian Schools, St. John was a dedicated and talented educator. He was always concerned with the education of poor children, establishing an institute to train other young men to be teachers. From this beginning came the Brothers of the

Christian Schools. Today, the Brothers of the Christian Schools are the largest religious institute of lay brothers, numbering some 8,000 worldwide. John Baptist de la Salle is credited also with being the first to create colleges devoted to teacher training; students were taught not in Latin but in the vernacular. His school at St.-Yon also served as the model for modern secondary education.

St. John Bosco (1815–1888) The founder of the Salesian order, Don Bosco wanted to be a priest from the age of nine. After ordination, he discovered thousands of children in his part of Italy in desperate need of education and care. So in a suburb of Turin, he opened a boarding house, followed by workshops where various trades such as shoemaking and tailoring were taught. From that beginning grew a congregation to advance Bosco's work, founded in 1859 and named by Bosco the Salesians after his deep admiration for St. Francis de Sales. In 1872, Bosco established a similar congregation for women near Genoa with St. Mary Mazzarello (d. 1881) called the Daughters of Mary, Help of Christians. By the time of his death, the congregation had nearly a thousand priests and some nine hundred sisters. He is a model for infinite patience and deep concern for children. Pope Pius XI said of him, "In his life the supernatural almost became natural and the extraordinary, ordinary."

St. John Chrysostom (c. 347–407) Bishop of Constantinople and a Doctor of the Church, John was called Chrysostom ("golden-mouthed") for his stunning eloquence, especially during homilies. He wanted to be a monk, but his health was always too poor. Finally ordained a priest, his preaching to the Christian community was so magnificent that he was offered the post of bishop of Constantinople. While the Byzantine people loved him and his calls for spiritual reform, the aristocracy greeted him with suspicion and resentment. Empress Eudoxia connived against him and secured his condemnation and eventually his exile to the wilderness. There he died from the cold and the harsh treatment of guards. His writings include the treatise *On the Priesthood*, and his spirituality is one of personal renewal by prayer and love.

St. John Climacus (c. 579–649) Also called John of the Ladder, John was a Byzantine ascetic, writer, and member of the famous monastery of St. Catherine in the Sinai. After spending time as a monk in the Sinai, he retired from monastic life to become a hermit. A beloved spiritual writer, he authored the *Ladder of Paradise* (or *Ladder of Divine Ascent*), a guide to the acquisition of Christian ideals of spiritual perfection. The book was divided into thirty chapters, each a step along the ladder, culminating with the divine union. Much of his style is unapproachable to modern audiences, but his words of contemplative union echo other great mystics, such as John of the Cross and Teresa of Ávila.

St. John of the Cross (1542–1591) One of the greatest mystics in the history of the Church, along with Teresa of Ávila, John is honored as the Doctor of Mystical Theology. A Spaniard, he entered the Carmelite order but was much troubled by the laxity he saw there. He thus received permission from his superiors to adhere privately to the rigorous life established by the original rule. His remaining life was devoted to promoting reform and writing, although his years were sorely troubled by run-ins with the Spanish Inquisition. He spent nine months trapped in a tiny cell in the monastery in Toledo by a group of Carmelites opposed to his reforms. He escaped by a makeshift rope and eventually won the separation of his followers, the Discalced Carmelites, from the rest of his order. His chief works are *Spiritual Canticle, Ascent of Mount Carmel, Living Flame of Love*, and *Dark Night of the Soul*. These are now spiritual classics by which John presented the stages of development of the human soul through purgation ("the night of the senses"), illumination ("the night of the spirit"), and the transforming union, the latter described in *Living Flame* with its accompanying commentary. With Teresa of Ávila and Francis de Sales, John is mandatory reading for those seeking the spiritual life and true mystical union with God. His writings are challenging and not easily understood by novices, but they represent one of the highest moments in the history of mysticism.

St. John Damascene (c. 675–749) The last of the Greek Fathers of the Church, John was an adviser to the caliph Abdul Malik, as chief representative of the Christian community (*Logothete*) to the caliph in Damascus. In 719, however, he was compelled to resign his post because of his Christian faith. He entered a monastery near Jerusalem, where he concentrated his energies on prayer and writing; he authored 150 works on theology, religious education, hagiographies, and philosophy. His two most famous writings were *Sacred Parallels* and *Fount of Wisdom*.

St. John Eudes (1601–1680) A French Jesuit and founder of the Sisters of Our Lady of Charity of Refuge and the Congregation of Jesus-Mary, St. John was also one of the first writers to promote devotion to the Sacred Hearts of Jesus and Mary with St. Margaret Mary Alacoque. During the terrible outbreak of plague, John was noted for his courageous care of victims, thereafter working as a missionary in the country. The order he founded, the Eudists, was nearly wiped out in the years of the French Revolution, but they were reconstituted in 1826 and continue to function as educators in South America, Europe, the United States, and Canada.

St. John of Kanty (1390–1473) Patron saint of Poland and Lithuania, John was a popular preacher and parish priest who spoke before thousands on how to be good Christians in a world full of violence and death. Famous for his austerities and care for the poor, he was declared a patron of Poland and Lithuania by Pope Clement XII in 1737 in recognition of the great love and interest he had in the people of both countries.

St. John Vianney (1786–1859) Called the Curé d'Ars, John Vianney is the patron of parish priests and one of history's great preachers and confessors. He seemed a poor choice for the priesthood, as he could barely master Latin and was considered rather dim. Once in ministry, however, people flocked to hear him preach, but above all to confess their sins and seek his advice. As time passed and his fame continued to spread, people arrived from other countries. He eventually spent eighteen hours a day in the confessional listening to the sins of tens of thousands of people. He earned the enmity of fellow priests who, dismissing him as ignorant, refused to accept the authenticity of his mission. When some complained that he was insane or mentally unstable, the local bishop replied that he wished all his priests had a touch of the same insanity.

Pope John Paul II (b. 1920–) Pope from 1978 and one of the foremost religious figures of the twentieth century, Karol Wojtyla was a native of Cracow, surviving first the Nazi occupation of Poland (1939–1945) and then cruel subjugation by the Communists. He rose rapidly through the Church, serving as auxiliary bishop and then archbishop of Cracow, cardinal, and finally pope as successor to Pope Paul VI. One of the longest reigning and most memorable pontiffs ever, John Paul II is also the most traveled pope ever and the most prolific. He has visited 130 countries, written 14 encyclicals, and canonized more than 460 saints. He also survived an assassination attempt in 1981 to preside over the greatest population increase of Catholics in Church history, while enjoying immense political and social influence by exhorting people everywhere to respect and nurture human rights and the innate dignity of the human person. His reign has been an exhortation for people everywhere to place their trust in God and "Be not afraid!"

St. Josemaría Escrivá de Balaguer (1902–1975) A Spanish priest, Josemaría founded Opus Dei, the modern Catholic society intended to promote holiness among individuals in the world. Initially begun for men, Opus Dei membership was expanded to women on February 14, 1930. Today, Opus Dei claims membership of nearly 2,000 priests, 355 major seminarians, and 82,000 lay persons—men and women, married and single, of every class and social condition—from 80 countries. Josemaría also authored *The Way,* one of the most popular devotional works in modern history; it has been published in 372 printings in 44 languages, with more than four and a half million copies in print. Much like St. Francis de Sales, Josemaría teaches that sanctity is not just for monks and hermits. Holiness is for everyone, and it is attainable in every walk of life and circumstance.

St. Joseph Cafasso (1811–1860) A famous Italian confessor, Joseph overcame a severely deformed spine to receive ordination. He was deeply respected as a spiritual adviser and was a good friend of St. John Bosco.

Julian of Norwich (c. 1342–after 1413) A renowned English mystic, Julian was the author of the famous work *Revelation of Divine Love*. Few details of her life are known save for the fact that she was an anchoress who spent her days in prayer. Starting in May 1373, she was the recipient of a series of visions concerning the Holy Trinity and the Passion. The *Revelation* details what she had seen, but wasn't written until some twenty years later. One of the most remarkable and profound works on mysticism, it stresses divine love as the source of ending all problems of existence. She should be read by anyone searching to understand God's love and how even one person can comprehend the wonders of creation.

Pope Julius III (d. 1555) Pope from 1550–1555 and a pope of the Catholic Reformation. Born Giovanni Maria Ciocchi del Monte, he enjoyed a rapid rise in the Church and served in 1545 as co-president and a papal legate to the Council of Trent. Aside from his zeal for reform in the Church, Julius was a lover of the arts; he named Michelangelo chief architect of St. Peter's and the gifted composer Palastrina the choirmaster.

Blessed Junípero Serra (1713–1784) One of the most famous missionaries in the history of the United States, Junípero Serra was a Spanish Franciscan who devoted most of his life to preaching the Catholic faith in California. Most of the famous missions of California—San Gabriel, San Luis Obispo, San Juan Capistrano, Santa Clara, and Santa Barbara (1782)—were all founded by his labors, and more than 5,000 native peoples of California were baptized into the faith at his hand. His spirituality has long been overlooked, in particular his unshakable confidence in the Providence of God.

Brother Lawrence (1611–1691) A French Carmelite, Brother Lawrence is best known for promoting the spirituality of "The Practice of the Presence of God." Originally Nicholas Herman of Lorraine, he served as a young man in the army. The horrors of war, however, led him to the life of a lay brother among the Carmelites. Years of prayer and meditation shaped his great spirituality, especially his keen insight into how to live in God's presence every moment of the day. He demonstrated such deep spiritual tranquility that others came to him for advice. After his death, his reflections were published and became a model for simple faith and living truly with God in our actions and our thoughts.

Pope St. Leo I the Great (d. 461) Pope from 440–461, he, along with St. Gregory I and Nicholas I are the only popes to date to receive the title "the Great." He served as pope during a terrible time, as the Roman Empire was dying in the West. The darkest moment came in 452, when Attila the Hun was poised to sack all of Italy. The pope bravely met him at Mantua and convinced him to withdraw. Three years later, the Vandals under King Geiseric arrived, and Leo greeted him at the gates of Rome. Although unable to prevent the sack of the city, he did win from Geiseric the promise not to burn or massacre. Of his many writings, 143 letters and 96 sermons survive, revealing a determined and prayerful personality.

Pope Leo X (d. 1521) Pope from 1513–1521, Leo was one of the most famous of the so-called Renaissance popes. A member of the de' Medici family, he was elected successor to the warrior pope Julius II at the age of thirty-eight. Sadly, he did little to encourage reform in the Church, and the Protestant Reformation began in Germany while he enjoyed banquets in Rome. He was famous for the declaration made at the start of his pontificate, "Let us enjoy the papacy which God has chosen to give us." Curiously, he was actually morally upright, remaining free of any personal scandals, save for his love of feasts and music at the expense of needed reform.

Pope Leo XIII (d. 1903) Pope from 1878–1903, Leo was the first pontiff of the twentieth century and the founder of Catholic social doctrine. Elected after the longest reign in Church history (Pope Pius IX served for thirty-two years), Leo was not expected to live long. Instead, he enjoyed twenty-five years of excellent health. In his encyclical *Rerum Novarum,* Leo forecast the concerns of the Church in the new century for the rights of workers and the dangers of both capitalism and communism.

Pope Liberius (d. 366) Pope from 352–366, Liberius was the first pontiff not honored as a saint. His time was troubled by the great heresy of Arianism, and for his refusal to condemn the enemy of the Arians, St. Athanasius, Liberius was banished from Rome for a time by Emperor Constantius II.

Blessed Louis Guanella (1842–1915) An Italian priest, Louis was a disciple of St. John Bosco and was, thus, deeply concerned for the welfare of poor and homeless children. To assist those labors, he founded two religious orders, the Servants of Charity and the Daughter of St. Mary. Both communities still continue to minister in Italy, the United States, and other countries. Father Guanella also visited the United States in 1912 to study the needs of the many Italian immigrants who were settling in America in large numbers. Known for his holiness even during his lifetime, the Church honored him in death beatifying him in 1964. His spirituality was a simple one of trust in God and working toward fulfilling one's vocation with love and zeal.

Chiara Lubich (1920–) An Italian educator and founder of the Focolare Movement, Chiara was working as an elementary school teacher in Trent during World War II when, on a night in 1943, her life was changed forever. After a night of terrible bombing, Chiara and a group of her friends realized that true social change could be accomplished only by living the Gospel. They cared for the poor and suffering, and found throughout Italy, Europe, and eventually the world many other men and women eager to join them. Today, the movement claims two million members and provides care for the poor in 182 countries. Chiara describes its aim in simple terms: "That all may be one—We were born for these words, for unity, to contribute towards its fulfillment in the world."

St. Madeleine Sophie Barat (d. 1865) The French foundress of the Society of the Sacred Heart of Jesus, Madeleine was devoted to the education of young people. Indeed, before her death, she personally established more than one hundred houses and schools in twelve countries.

Raïssa Maritain (1883–1960) The wife of the celebrated philosopher Jacques Maritain and a brilliant writer in her own right, Raissa Maritain was born in Russia to a Jewish family. She met Jacques while studying in Paris and shared with him her own frustrations at being an atheist. They married in 1904 and gradually journeyed together to the Church, becoming Catholics in 1906. Inspired by the writings of the Christian mystics, she often visited a contemplative convent, Regina Laudis in Bethleham, Connecticut, while her husband was teaching at Princeton. She was a poet, writer, true intellectual, and woman of rich spiritual insights. Raissa is a model for young women seeking faith, spiritual maturity, and the truth that belief is possible in the modern world.

St. Mark the Ascetic (fl. fifth century) A hermit and disciple of St. John Chrysostom, St. Mark is also known as Mark the Wrestler and Mark the Hermit. Little is known about the details of his life, but he is the presumed author of more than 200 works concerning Spiritual Law, baptism, penance, and grace. He may have been the abbot of a monastery at Ancyra (modern Ankara, Turkey), but he gave up his office to become a desert hermit. According to custom, he knew every passage of Scripture by heart and once supposedly cured a blind hyena.

St. Mary Magdalen de' Pazzi (d. 1607) An Italian Discalced Carmelite and mystic, Mary experienced numerous ecstasies and five years of spiritual aridity. She performed miracles of healing and was also reputed to be able to read people's mind. She died after three years of almost ceaseless spiritual and physical suffering. Mary is a model for anyone who is enduring suffering, desolation, or struggles of the spirit.

St. Mary Mazzarello (1837–1881) An Italian nun, Mary was the co-founder of the Daughters of Mary, Help of Christians with St. John Bosco. After entering the Daughters of Mary Immaculate at the age of fifteen, she suffered a bout of typhoid, an episode that made her aware forever after of her absolute dependence upon God. She was thus advanced in the spiritual life when Don Bosco chose her in 1872 to help him found the Institute of the Daughters of Mary, Help of Christians. She proved a talented superior, teacher, and spiritual mother to the new institute, and the community she founded soon multiplied. Her spirituality was in the long tradition of other masters such as de Caussaude in her abandonment of the self into God's hands even while working actively in the world to achieve holiness.

St. Maximus the Confessor (c. 580–662) A Byzantine theologian, Maximus is revered as a martyr for opposing the Byzantine Emperor

Constans II. At first banished from capital, Maximus was dragged back to the imperial Constantinople in 661. He once again refused to yield, and so his tongue and right hand were chopped off and numerous humiliations were heaped upon him. Banished to the area around the Black Sea, he died on August 13, 662. Maximus is honored with the title of "The Theologian" and is ranked as a Doctor for his contributions to the theology of the Incarnation. The author of some ninety works on theology, mysticism, and dogma, his theological brilliance was displayed in such writings as his *Opuscula theologica et polemica* (*Short Theological and Polemical Treatises*); the *Ambigua* on Gregory of Nazianzus; and the *Mystagogia,* a study on symbolism that was an important entry in liturgical literary history.

St. Mechtild of Magdeburg (1210–c. 1285) A famous German mystic, Mechtild experienced a mystical visitation from the Holy Spirit at the age of twelve. Over the next several years, she received many other visions, and, at the order of her spiritual director, undertook to write them down. Her visions were recorded in the book generally known as *Das fleissende Licht der Gottheit*, derived from the title God purportedly had declared for it, *Vliessende licht miner gotheit in allu die herzen die da lebent ane valscheit* (*Light of My Divinity, Flowing Into All Hearts That Live Without Guile*). *Das fleissende* had a lasting impression on later German mysticism.

Thomas Merton (1915–1968) One of the most popular spiritual writers of the twentieth century, Thomas Merton was also a poet, theologian, and a longtime member of the Trappists. Orphaned at the age of sixteen, he wandering for a time in France and England and then won a scholarship to Cambridge (1933–1934). Dismissed after only one year because of his improper lifestyle and lack of discipline, he went to America, attended Columbia University, and earned a bachelor's in literature and poetry in 1937 and then a master's in 1939. Baptized into the Church in 1938, he underwent a profound conversion and in 1941 entered the Trappist Abbey of Our Lady of Gethsemane, near Bardstown, Kentucky. In 1965, however, he was allowed by the community to adopt a solitary lifestyle away from the abbey itself. He lived in a small house in the adjoining hills where he studied and focused on the mystical life. His interest in Eastern mysticism and philosophy led to a tour of Asia, where he met with numerous Eastern religious leaders, including the Dalai Lama. While in Bangkok, Thailand, he died by accidental electrocution while bathing.

Merton first achieved international fame for his autobiographical account of his spiritual journey to the Trappists, *The Seven Storey Mountain* (1948). Among his other important works were *Ascent to Truth* (1951), *Mystics and Zen Masters, No Man Is an Island* (1955), and *Faith and Contemplation* (1962). He should be read by those who feel spiritually lost in the modern world.

Michelangelo (1475–1564) Michelangelo Buonarroti was not only one of the foremost of all Renaissance artists, he was a true Renaissance genius. A few of his most famous works as a sculptor were the *Pietà, Moses,* and *David;* as an architect, he was chief designer of the Dome of St. Peter's Basilica and a brilliant engineer for the city of Florence; as a painter, he created the masterpiece of the Sistine Chapel and the *Last Judgment*. Michelangelo was also a poet and writer of immense depth and faith, although he was always tortured by his own artistic and spiritual shortcomings. He is a model for those hoping to transform every worthy endeavor into moments of prayer and to make them gifts of thanks to God for talents, energy, and time.

Emmanuel Mounier (1905–1950) A French philosopher, Mounier exercised considerable influence over modern philosophy through his development of the idea of personalism. In this approach, he argued in favor of the person in contrast to the individual. Mounier's emphasis on the value of the person has been an antidote to a modern world so willing to suppress the human spirit. His writings are a powerful fusion of Catholicism and democracy; fellow philosopher Paul Ricœur termed his work the "matrix of philosophies."

John Henry Cardinal Newman (1801–1890) The most famous English Catholic convert and one of the greatest minds of the nineteenth century, Newman journeyed from atheism to Catholicism, eventually gaining membership in the Sacred College of Cardinals. The son of a London banker, Newman announced one day at school his total disbelief in God. His schoolmaster, however, persuaded him to read John Calvin and the Bible. What followed was a long road to faith that included ordination as an Anglican deacon and his conversion to Catholicism in 1845. He was ordained a priest and gained an international following for his writings. For anyone wandering through the dark wilderness of doubt seeking the light of faith, Newman's autobiography, *Apologia pro vita sua* (1864), offers a valuable lesson in how successful that journey can be. For those seeking to deepen their understanding of how a soul can find God, Newman gave us the poem "The Dream of Gerontius" (1866). Newman is also someone from whom we draw strength to defend what we believe. We can take inspiration from his personal motto: "*Ex umbris et imaginibus in veritatem*" ("Out of the shadows and images into the truth").

Pope Nicholas I (d. 867) Pope from 858–867, Nicholas has been called "the Great" because of how he dominated the medieval landscape. He involved himself in many temporal affairs in order to assist with what he saw were the needs of the Church. His efforts made the popes much stronger in the years to come and made it possible for his successors to deal with the many political leaders who sought to dominate the Church.

Nicholas von Flüe (1417–1487) A Swiss mystic and ascetic, Nicholas was originally a judge, scholar, and soldier, fighting in two wars on behalf of his native land. Married to a woman named Dorothy, he fathered ten children. In 1465, however, he retired from public life and then, in 1467, he gave up his family to become a hermit. In a time filled with war, plagues, and uncertainty, he offered powerful spiritual advice and inspiration. Around 1481, he was consulted by leading political figures in Switzerland, who hoped he might prevent a Swiss civil war. His suggestions were soon adopted, and peace was achieved.

Henri Nouwen (1932–1996) A Dutch priest and popular spiritual writer, Nouwen coined the popular term "wounded healer" to describe the role and the task of those engaged in ministry. Drawn to the priesthood from the age of eight, he became a priest and specialized in psychology. Over the next decades he held teaching positions at Notre Dame, Yale, and Harvard; was a missionary in Bolivia and Peru; and in 1986, agreed to serve as pastor for L'Arche Daybreak, a community in Canada for the care of mentally and physically handicapped people. A sensitive writer, Nouwen always stressed that we are imperfect people, but Christ can touch and transform the lives of others through us. He also taught the central value of promoting hospitality—(an authentic welcome offered to everyone to experience our warmth, generosity, and gift of self). His most popular book was *The Wounded Healer*.

Flannery O'Connor (1925–1964) A Southern writer, O'Connor died from lupus at the age of thirty-nine and left a literary legacy of only two novels, thirty-two short stories, and various reviews and commentaries. Nevertheless, she is ranked as one of the foremost literary figures in twentieth-century American literature. Her writing style was both comic and brutal, and her stories were full of shockingly memorable and even violent characters, bringing decadent Southern culture to life. Her work also contained a great Catholic depth, as expressed in her essay "The Catholic Novelist in the Protestant South" (1969) and *The Habit of Being* (1979), in which she discussed the influence of Catholicism on her life and writings. O'Connor's short stories are considered her foremost work, including "A Good Man Is Hard to Find," "The Geranium," "A View of the Woods," and "Good Country People."

Blaise Pascal (1623–1662) A French mathematician, physicist, and apologist, Pascal was a deeply religious individual in an age increasingly losing its spiritual interests. He is best known for two works, *Pensées* (*Thoughts*; 1670), a collection of his thoughts in the form of notes; and *Lettres provincials* (*Provincial Letters*, 1656–1657), a series of letters attacking the Jesuits. Although he was an iconoclast who thought humans were virtually incapable of goodness because of our fallen nature, he nevertheless offered rich insights into the human soul. In his typically pragmatic outlook, he devised what has been called Pascal's wager—one makes a wager in believing in God, for if there is a God one has chosen wisely; if there is no God nothing has been lost.

Pope Paul VI (1897–1978) Pope from 1963–1978, Giovanni Battista Montini is best known for completing the work begun by his predecessor, Pope John XXIII, at the Second Vatican Council (1962–1965). His long, subsequent pontificate was taken up with trying to steer the Church toward authentic implementation of the many documents, decrees, and reforms of the council. In diplomatic matters, he labored to reduce tension between the Church and the Communists of Eastern European countries by means of a detente type of policy called *Ostpolitik*. He was also the first pope in many centuries to visit the Holy Land. In 1968 he instituted the annual observance of a World Day of Peace on New Year's Day to offer a message of peace to all the world's political leaders and the peoples of all nations. A deeply spiritual priest, Paul suffered much sadness because of the violence that took place during his reign, including the murder of Italian premier Aldo Moro just before his own death.

St. Paul (d. c. 64 or 67) The so-called Apostle to the Gentiles, Paul is one of the most influential writers, missionaries, and theologians in the history of the Church. Born at Tarsus and a Roman citizen, he participated in the persecution of Christians until the time of his miraculous and renowned conversion on the way to Damascus. Called by Christ, Paul was completely converted, taking the Gospel message across much of the Roman Empire, including Palestine, Cyprus, Asia Minor, Greece, and even Rome. He authored a quarter of the New Testament—fourteen epistles bear his name—and his impact is still felt today. Like other disciples of the early Church, he was martyred—beheaded just outside the walls of Rome during the persecutions by Emperor Nero.

St. Peter (d. c. 64 or 65) The first pope and the prince of the Apostles, Simon, son of Jonah, was a fisherman at the time of his calling by Christ. Declared Cephas or Peter (the Rock) by Christ, he was made chief of the Apostles and head of the Church, as is clear throughout the Synoptic Gospels and the Acts of the Apostles. Tough, headstrong, and very practical, he was the first Christian to preach the Gospel in and around Jerusalem after Pentecost and was the unquestioned leader of the first Christian community there. He later established his see in Rome, where he spent his last years and was martyred by crucifixion in 64 or 65 during the Neronian persecution. According to tradition, he was crucified upside down by the obliging Romans after declaring that he was unworthy to die in the same manner as Christ.

St. Peter of Alcantara (1499–1562) A Spanish mystic and the founder of the Discalced Franciscans of Spain, Peter was an ardent reformer, much like his contemporaries, St. Teresa of Ávila and St. John of the Cross. He was also reputed to be a brilliant spiritual adviser. He was especially important in encouraging St. Teresa of Ávila in her attempted reforms of the Carmelite order and in her establishing the monastery of Ávila in 1562. St. Teresa's autobiography is the main source on Peter's life and gifts. Although almost forgotten today, his writings were very popular in the seventeenth century.

St. Peter Julian Eymard (1811–1868) The founder of the Congregation of the Priests of the Blessed Sacrament, Peter took as his chief life's work promoting the adoration of the Blessed Sacrament. Everything he did was geared toward that, including starting his own order. He also founded a second order, for women, receiving encouragement throughout from St. John Vianney.

St. Philip Neri (1515–1595) An Italian priest, Philip founded the Congregation of the Oratory, a religious community that later claimed Cardinal John Henry Newman as a member. He is honored as the second apostle of Rome because of the years he devoted to missionary in the Eternal City. While a Catholic city, Philip found that there was a need for the Gospel to be preached anew among the Romans, demonstrating that the faith must be even renewed and encouraged even in places and among people considered safely within the community of faith.

St. Padre Pio (1887–1968) A world famous Franciscan friar and stigmatic, Padre Pio of Pietrelcina entered at the age of sixteen. Ordained in 1910, he was sent to the friary of San Giovanni

Rotondo in 1916 and remained there until his death. He soon earned notoriety for his spiritual gifts and discernment and was especially devoted to prayer, declaring, "In books we seek God, in prayer we find him. Prayer is the key which opens God's heart." In assisting the thousands who came to him for counsel, he demonstrated to an exemplary degree the virtue of prudence, acting and counseling in the light of God. Among those he met over his decades of service was Karol Wojtyla, the future Pope John Paul II. Pope John Paul II declared him a saint in 2002. More than 300,000 people crammed into St. Peter's Square in sweltering 90-degree heat to attend the canonization.

Pope St. Pius X (1835–1914) Pope from 1903 to 1914 and the last pope to be canonized a saint, Pius was born Giuseppe Melchior Sarto, the son of a postman and a seamstress. Although considered holy and deeply pastoral, he was not considered a favorite going into the conclave to elect a new pope in 1903. It was, thus, a major surprise when the cardinals chose the patriarch of Venice. Sarto accepted only upon the insistence of the other cardinals.

Taking the name Pius and adopting the motto *Instaurare omnia in Christo* ("To restore all things in Christ") Pius brought to the Holy See the same pastoral devotion that characterized his career. Among his concerns as pope were promoting daily Communion, the reform of Church music, and trying to stop the eruption of World War I. Typical of his outlook, it was said that after his election he was shown the papal apartments, including his bed; upon seeing the mattress, he sighed and commented, "It is beautiful, but I will die in it."

Pope Pius XI (d. 1939) Pope from 1922–1939, Ambrogio Damiano Achille Ratti was the son of a manager of a silk factory. After a brilliant career in Rome, he was elected pope to succeed Pope Benedict XV after being appointed a cardinal a mere seven months before. Pius took as his motto, "To seek the peace of Christ through the reign of Christ," and throughout his pontificate he was an advocate of peace in a world heading toward global disaster and war. Aside from his diplomatic efforts and concerns for the Church, Pius sought to encourage holiness in the world by a number of major canonizations, including Thérèse of Lisieux, John Fisher, Thomas More, Bernadette Soubirous, and John Bosco; Robert Bellarmine, John of the Cross, Albertus Magnus, and Peter Canisius were made Doctors of the Church.

Pope Pius XII (d. 1958) Pope from 1939–1958, Eugenio Maria Giuseppe Giovanni Pacelli served as pontiff throughout the Second World War and set the stage for the Second Vatican Council. Elected on the eve of World War II, Pius worked unsuccessfully to prevent the outbreak of violence and spent the next six years trying to maintain a position of neutrality in the long war and speaking out in favor of peace. He also devoted all his available resources to ease the suffering of refugees through the Pontifical Aid Commission. He has been attacked in recent years for not doing more to prevent the Holocaust, but he has also been defended by scholars all over the world, including many Jewish historians. In perhaps the most memorable moment of Pius's pontificate, he greeted the Allied army that liberated Rome in the summer of 1944, transfixing the soldiers and jubilant people who flooded St. Peter's Square to celebrate the city's freedom. Many post-war reforms launched by Pope Pius helped lay the foundation for the sweeping changed enacted under Popes John XXIII (r. 1958–1963) and Paul VI (1963–1978).

Blessed Rafaela Mary Porras (1850–1925) A native of Spain, Rafaela established the Handmaids of the Sacred Heart, devoted to teaching children and rendering all possible assistance to those organizing spiritual retreats. Rafaela resigned as head of her own foundation in 1893 and spent the rest of her life anonymously in the congregation's house in Rome. Her spirituality was one of placing her work for God before personal ambition and desire for credit.

Hugo Rahner (1900–1968) A Jesuit theologian, Hugo Rahner was the lesser-known brother of the famed theologian Karl Rahner. His own interests extended across the spectrum of theology, and he authored a number of notable books, including *Church and State in Early Christianity*, *Greek Myths and Christian Mystery*, *Ignatius the Theologian*, and *The Spirituality of St. Ignatius Loyola: An Account of Its Historical Development*.

Rainer Maria Rilke (1875–1926) A German writer and poet, Rilke is considered one of the greatest lyric poets of modern Germany. His youth was troubled greatly by the demands of his mother, who forced him to wear dresses until the age of five to make up for the death of a daughter a few years before. Rilke emerged as one of Europe's foremost poets, with such works as *The Book of Hours: The Book of Monastic Life, The Duino Elegies*, and

Sonnets to Orpheus. The latter two were much concerned with "the oneness of life and death." He also maintained a remarkable correspondence with Auguste Rodin, André Gide, H. V. Hofmannstahl, and Boris Pasternak. In his last years, Rilke lived in Switzerland. He suffered from leukemia, and died, it has been said, of an infection he contracted when he pricked himself on a rose thorn.

St. Rita of Cascia (1381–1457) An Italian widow, Rita lived for most of her life as a cloistered Augustinian nun in Umbria and has long been invoked as a patron of those facing impossible or desperate situations. She was forced by her family to marry, despite her personal wishes to be a nun, and for eighteen years she was devoted to her husband and children. Her husband, however, was abusive and cruel, and his death, coupled with the fact that her children had grown up, permitted her finally to enter the religious life. Her years as a nun were noted for her devotion to prayer and her austerities. Her spirituality has always been one of patience and fortitude in terrible personal situations, even those that seem to have no foreseeable end or hope.

St. Robert Bellarmine (1542–1621) A cardinal, theologian, and leader of the Catholic Reformation, Robert Bellarmine was one of Catholicism's most ardent defenders. He was also a brilliant controversialist against the Protestants during the Protestant Reformation, providing a famous definition of the Catholic Church: "The one and true Church is the assembly of men, bound together by the profession of the same sacraments, under the rule of legitimate pastors, and in particular the see of the Vicar of Christ on earth, the Roman Pontiff."

Blessed Robert Southwell (1561–1595) A Jesuit missionary, poet, and martyr, Robert was born in England but studied on the Continent because there were no Catholic schools in the British Isles. Ordained to the Jesuits, he returned to England in 1586 and secretly labored as a priest among English Catholics. Finally arrested in 1592, he was tried in 1595 for treason and executed by being hanged and quartered. Southwell was a popular poet, penning such notable works as "Triumphs over Death," "The Burning Babe," "Short Rule of Good Life," "Hundred Meditations," and his longest poem, "St. Peter's Complaint." He was much respected by later religious poets and earned the admiration of Ben Johnson.

St. Rose Duchesne (d. 1852) The French founding nun of the Society of the Sacred Heart, Rose-Philippine fulfilled a life's dream in 1818 when she arrived in New Orleans and began missionary work. Going to St. Charles, Missouri, she founded the first convent of the Society in the United States and soon began a school for girls. In the coming years, she launched six more mission stations and worked as a missionary to Native Americans. Although a saint, she is almost forgotten today in the United States.

Antoine de St.-Exupéry (1900–1944) Poet, pilot, and writer, much like his character in the story of *The Little Prince,* St.-Exupéry loved to fly, so much so that he became pilot of mail service from Toulouse to Dakar and flew all over Africa. In 1938, he moved to the United States and used his long experience in the air in his writings, including *Night Flight* (*Vol de Nuit*, 1931), *Southern Mail* (*Courrier Sud*, 1929), *Flight to Arras* (*Pilote de Guerre*, 1942) *Airman's*

Odyssey, Wisdoms of the Sands, Letter to a Hostage (Letter à un Otage, 1943) and *Wind, Sand and Stars (Terre des Hommes,* 1939). His best-known work was *The Little Prince (Le Petit Prince),* written in New York City in 1940. The gentle tale of a lost prince is one of the most-read books of the twentieth century. St.-Exupéry died as he lived—in the air. Fighting to free his beloved France from Nazi occupation, he was shot down during a mission the Mediterranean.

Christoph Cardinal Schönborn (1945–) An Austrian cardinal and theologian, Cardinal Schönborn entered the Dominicans in 1963 and was ordained a priest in 1970. He soon distinguished himself as one of the most talented young theologians in Europe, earning a key role in the drafting of the *Catechism of the Catholic Church.* Appointed the archbishop of Vienna in 1995, he was faced with the difficult task of restoring the unity of the Church in Austria after the former cardinal resigned for impropriety. His writings are noted for the gentle eloquence, especially his expressive style in describing the nature of the Church.

Blessed Sebastian Valfre (1629–1710). A priest of the Oratory in Turin, Sebastian is honored as the patron of Inner City Pastors, those priests and ministers dedicated to caring for people in the crowded and dangerous bowels of our major cities. He joined the Oratorians at Turin immediately after his ordination and proved a talented spiritual adviser and pastor. Unlike other priests, however, he did not merely aid those who came to him. He set out to find the sick, the helpless, and the lost. He brought comfort and faith to thousands. Throughout his long life, Sebastian also displayed almost ceaseless joy in his ministry, even in the midst of the horrors of the plague-filled and squalid quarters of Turin.

Fr. Antoine Sertillanges, O.P. (1863–1948) A French Dominican theologian and philosopher, Fr. Sertillanges held a professorship in moral philosophy at the Catholic Institute of Paris. His specialization was in Thomism, and Sertillanges was a member and ardent supporter of the so-called Neo-Scholastic Movement, the effort in the late nineteenth century and early twentieth century to promote a renewal of Scholastic theology. This gifted priest is also remembered for his commitment to authentic Christian humanism, foreshadowing the Church's efforts in the twentieth century to defend the rights and dignity of the human person.

Archbishop Fulton J. Sheen (1895–1979) An archbishop and, during the 1950s, one of the most popular religious leaders in the United States, Fulton Sheen is also ranked as perhaps the most superbly educated and eloquent apologists for the Catholic faith in American history. Born in El Paso, Illinois, he entered the seminary; studied in Louvain, the Sorbonne, and in England; and earned several doctorates in philosophy and theology. He swiftly emerged as a photogenic and erudite spokesman for Catholic teachings: His television program *Life Is Worth Living* was the number-one show in the country during the early 1950s, smashing Milton Berle's own beloved show. (Berle did not complain, though, as he said Sheen had better writers—Matthew, Mark, Luke, and John.) Sheen also appeared on the cover of *Time* magazine and won an Emmy.

Bernadette Soubirous (1844–1879) A simple French peasant girl, Bernadette is beloved for being the recipient of a series of visions of the Blessed Virgin at Lourdes in 1858. At the time of the apparitions, Bernadette was considered a pleasant and innocent person but also backward and uneducated. After eighteen visitations, the phenomenon stopped and Bernadette was forced to endure the rigorous examination of the Church and the even more difficult scrutiny and insensitivity of the public. In 1866, she entered the Sisters of Notre Dame at Nevers. Her health, always weak, soon deteriorated, and she died on April 16, 1879, after horrifying suffering from tuberculosis of the bone. Lourdes, meanwhile, emerged as one of the foremost pilgrim sites in Christendom, a development that took place entirely without impetus from Bernadette. She is a model for those seeking spiritual advancement through humility and obedience to God's will.

St. Stephen of Hungary (977–1038) The patron saint of Hungary and first king of that country, Stephen was originally the son of a Magyar chieftain. Raised a Christian, he devoted his life to promoting Christianity in Hungary, building churches, encouraging the religious life, and defending Church rights. His crown and regalia became beloved symbols of the Hungarian nation, and Stephen was venerated as the ideal Christian king.

Pope Sylvester II (d. 1003) Pope from 999–1003, Sylvester was the first Frenchman to be elected pontiff. A great scholar and statesman, he worked as pope to curb simony and clerical marriages and to strengthen the Church in Hungary and Poland; he traditionally sent the famed Crown of St. Stephen to the Hungarian monarch in 1000. Sylvester also promoted education and was himself renowned for his knowledge of astronomy, mathematics, science, and Latin.

Mother Teresa (1910–1997) A sister, foundress, and Nobel Prize winner, Mother Teresa devoted her entire life to the care of the "poorest of the poor" in India and around the globe. Born Agnes Gonxha Bojaxhiu, the daughter of an Albanian grocer, she originally belonged to the congregation of Irish Loretto Sisters and was sent to India to teach the daughters of prosperous families. After a number of years, however, she asked permission to give up her teaching and devote herself to caring for the poor of the city. Granted approval by the authorities, she adopted the sari as her dress and, barefooted, began tending to the sick, teaching the children of the slums, and caring for the dying so as to allow them to pass into the next life with dignity. So began the Order of the Missionaries of Charity, now one of the most famous religious communities in the world and serving in more than thirty countries, including Great Britain, Australia, and the United States. Mother Teresa has progressed toward sainthood in almost record time and will probably be beatified soon.

St. Teresa of Ávila (1515–1582) One of the foremost mystics and theologians in the history of the Catholic Church, Teresa labored for many years to bring reform to the Carmelite Order of Nuns, facing the dangers of prison by her opponents. She never wavered in her commitment, however, because she rooted everything she did in her total love of God. She was so well traveled that she was given the nickname "the roving nun."

Although honored as a Doctor of the Church (the highest honor possible for any theologian), Teresa remains one of the most approachable thinkers you will ever meet. Rather than writing obscure theological tomes, she placed her spiritual gifts at anyone's disposal through her remarkable common sense and humor. She also proved that a mystic can live and work in the world. Her greatest books—such as her *Autobiography* (1565), *The Way of Perfection* (1573), and the *Interior Castle* (1577)—were written to help others on their way to God. Teresa can be a good friend to anyone who wants to love God but who finds it difficult to make the time. She provides a loving reminder that there is always time for God.

Tertullian (c. 160–c. 222) A Roman apologist, theologian, and controversialist, Tertullian was the son of a Roman soldier and raised as a pagan. Appalled by the state of social decay, he was drawn to Christianity and was attracted especially by the steadfastness of the Christian martyrs in the face of death. Once established in the Church, he authored a vast number of works, although in his later years he spent time with a heretical sect. Nevertheless, his immense contributions earned him the title of Father of Latin Theology and influenced the theological life of the Western Church for the next millennium. Among Tertullian's many famous quotes was his comment to Roman authorities that, "The blood of the martyrs is the seed of the Church." As with Newman and Hilaire—although centuries removed—Tertullian offers the modern reader a powerful means of learning how to defend the faith.

St. Thérèse of Lisieux (1873–1897) Called the Little Flower, St. Thérèse of the Child Jesus was a Carmelite nun, mystic, and a Doctor of the Church since 1997. Born in Normandy, France, she entered the Carmelite convent of Lisieux in Normandy at the age of fifteen and survived only nine more years. Before succumbing to tuberculosis, she endured severe personal struggles in her prayer life while maintaining the outward plainness of an ordinary nun. She engaged in daily work, prayer, and devotion, but she suffered terribly from doubts, isolation, and scruples. Nevertheless, she adhered steadfastly to the "little way"—placing her trust completely in God as a child loves and trusts a parent. Before her death, Thérèse had been instructed by her superiors to write an autobiography. Her work, *The Story of a Soul*, has since become one of the great spiritual works in Church history. Canonized in 1925, she was also honored as a patroness of France with Joan of Arc and a patron of the Catholic missions. One of the most beloved saints of the modern era, Thérèse is recognized as a powerful sign to people of all ages, but especially the young. She shows that even an ordinary, plain, and apparently insignificant person can achieve sanctity by fulfilling duties out of a perfect love for God, in matters great and small.

Thomas à Kempis (c. 1380–1471) An ascetic writer and probably the author of *Imitation of Christ,* Thomas was much influenced by the spiritual movement of the Brethren of the Common Life, becoming a monk and then a priest. A gifted preacher and spiritual adviser, he was especially fond of preaching the mystery of the Redemption and Christ's passion. A portrait of him at Getruidenberg bears his favorite motto, "Everywhere I have sought rest and found it nowhere, save in tiny nooks with tiny books." Thomas is believed by most scholars to be the author of *Imitatio Christi*, a manual of spiritual perfection, first circulated in 1418 and divided into four parts: Useful Admonitions for a Spiritual Life, Admonitions Concerning Interior Things, Interior Consolation, and the Blessed Sacrament. *Imitation* is ideal for anyone who needs or desires structure in their approach to the spiritual life. Virtually the entire journey to spiritual perfection is contained in the pages of this tiny book.

St. Thomas More (1478–1535) Lord Chancellor of England, humanist, scholar, and one of the most famous martyrs, Thomas More gave up his career, his power, and even his life because he would not sacrifice his faith. A member of the great humanist circle of Europe that boasted the likes of Erasmus and William Grocyn, More was the author of such famed works as *Utopia*. A brilliant criticism of contemporary English society, *Utopia* offers a fictional island nation called Utopia, where an ideal republic exists that is governed by the natural law. A friend of King Henry VIII, More was named in 1529 to serve as chancellor of England. He resigned in 1532 because of his irreconcilable opposition to the king's divorce from Catherine of Aragon. The king then persecuted him relentlessly, finally sending him to the Tower of London and beheading him on July 6, 1535. More is the ideal for anyone facing trials and persecution for their conscience.

St. Thomas of Villanova (1486–1555) The archbishop of Valencia, Thomas was called the Father of the Poor, serving as a spiritual patriarch for the entire city. As archbishop, he worked tirelessly for the people, founding a college for poor students, saying Mass every day for the workers, rebuilding the city's hospital after it was burned, closing prisons, and establishing a home for orphaned or abandoned infants. Thomas spent large sums to feed the hungry who came to his door and sent out his assistants to give money and aid to any who might need them. He is a model for generosity without pretense.

St. Vincent Pallotti (d. 1850) An Italian founder and priest. Born in Rome in 1798, he was the son of a grocer and was ordained at the age of twenty-three. He earned a doctorate in theology and taught in Rome for a time but then served as a parish priest in several parishes in the city. Enduring constant humiliations at the hands of his fellow curates and undergoing many personal austerities, he began apostolic work to organize both the clergy and laity for the promotion of social justice and personal conversion. Thus, in 1835, he established the Society of the Catholic Apostolate (known for a time as the Pious Society of Missions)—the Pallottines. From a humble beginning of only twelve members during his life, the Apostolate spread across the world. Vincent also worked to teach the poor, was a noted confessor and exorcist, and actively promoted the restoration of the Catholic faith in England. In 1836, he began the special observance of the Octave of the Epiphany to bring about the eventual reunion of the Orthodox Church with Rome. He was canonized in 1963.

St. Vincent De Paul (c. 1580–1660) One of the great patrons of the poor, Vincent was a priest and founder of the Lazarist Fathers and the Sisters of Charity. In 1605, while on a journey, his ship was captured by Barbary pirates. Taken into slavery, Vincent spent two hard years as a slave, finally escaping in 1607 to France. Subsequently ordained, he devoted his life to charitable work, establishing confraternities of men and women to bring comfort and hope to the poor and to care for the vast numbers of sick in Paris. His chief source of charitable donations and concerns came from wealthy noblewomen who provided funds for the creation of hospitals and homes for orphaned and foundling children. To advance his efforts even further, in 1625, Vincent founded in Paris the Congregation of the Missions, called the Lazarists or Vincentians, a society of priests with the express task of missionary labor and the training of clergy. St. Vincent stands with Mother Teresa as a guide for spiritual progress through selfless love of the forgotten and the poorest of the poor. Their road is not an easy one, but it is one of the most transforming.

Hans Urs von Balthasar (1905–1988) A Swiss theologian, cardinal, and founder of the journal *Communio,* von Balthasar ranks among the great theologians of the twentieth century, along with Henri de Lubac, Yves Congar, Karl Rahner, and Joseph Ratzinger. A member of the Jesuits, he was the author of an enormous body of writings that addressed the need to present the faith in terms comprehensible to the modern world. For his many contributions, von Balthasar was named a cardinal by Pope John Paul II just before his death. For seekers, von Balthasar encouraged the use of imagination in prayer, picturing the events of Christ's life in the mind as a means of cultivating our relationship with him.

Simone Weil (1909–1943) A French moral and political philosopher, teacher, and activist, Simone Weil was also a mystic deeply concerned with religious experience. From an early age, she felt an affinity with workers, actually giving up her life as a teacher to join the laborers in a factory. She critiqued both Marxism and capitalism and then underwent a profound spiritual conversion while listening to the chanting of monks at Solesmes Monastery. She wrote, "Christ himself came down and He took me," and then devoted herself to exploring the religious experience in essays, journals, and letters that served as the basis for her book *Waiting on God*. Weil stresses the power of martyrdom, sacrifice, and asceticism as a means of embracing the Christian life. Her spirituality made her one of the most expressive—if not misunderstood—mystics and activists of the twentieth century; her forms of sacrifice and mortification hastened her early death from tuberculosis and malnutrition while working for the Free French during World War II.